THE ONEIDA MAN

Conversations with my
Native American Friend

WEAM NAMOU

HERMiZ
PUBLiSHING

Copyright © 2023 by Weam Namou

All rights reserved. No part of this book may be reproduced or transmitted in any form or by any means, electronic or mechanical, including photocopying, recording or by any information storage and retrieval system, without permission from the author.

Library of Congress Cataloging-in-Publication Data
2023916458

Namou, Weam

ISBN: 978-1-945371-03-5 (paperback)

The Oneida Man
Conversations with my Native American Friend
(Creative Nonfiction)

First Edition

Published in the United States of America by:
Hermiz Publishing, Inc.
Sterling Heights, MI

10 9 8 7 6 5 4 3 2 1

THE ONEIDA MAN

Conversations with my Native American Friend

A Hermiz Publishing Book

CONTENTS

Books by Weam Namou vii

Acknowledgements ix

Introduction xi

Chapter 1: The Oneida Man 1

Chapter 2: Holly Wood Makes Very Good Wands 9

Chapter 3: Cleopatra's Dance Of Darkness 25

Chapter 4: At The Junkyard 32

Chapter 5: Dying, Again And Again 41

Chapter 6: Sleeping Bear Dunes 56

Chapter 7: The Worlds Of Corn And Honey 65

Chapter 8: Twenty-Year-Old Journal Entry 80

Chapter 9: The Ten Commandments 86

Chapter 10: Jesus Was Here 99

Chapter 11: The North American 108

Chapter 12: New Beginnings 122

Notes 133

BOOKS BY WEAM NAMOU

The Feminine Art

The Mismatched Braid

The Flavor of Cultures

I Am a Mute Iraqi with a Voice

The Great American Family

Iraqi Americans: The War Generation

Iraqi Americans: Witnessing a Genocide

Iraqi Americans: The Lives of the Artists

Healing Wisdom for a Wounded World

Mesopotamian Goddesses

Pomegranate

Little Baghdad

Healing Wisdom for a Wounded World
(Book 1 through Book 4)

ACKNOWLEDGEMENTS

To all the Native Americans who have generously shared with me their time and wisdom and entrusted me with their stories.

INTRODUCTION

I don't remember the first time I met my Native American friend. He remembers me from when he would come into my brother's party store, Avon Food Center. The store sat at the corner of Auburn and Ryan Road in Shelby Township, Michigan. I was then a teenager and fairly new to the United States. He was a customer, over thirteen years my senior, who bought a pack of cigarettes, a slice of pizza, and whatnot.

The initial store had a small shelf of VHS (Video Home System) rentals and a kitchen with a few dining tables. Years later, it moved across the street to a new shopping center. The new building included a party store, video store, pizzeria, tailor shop, and dry cleaner. I eventually worked at the video store for twelve years. During this time, my native friend came in to rent a movie after he stopped at the next-door store. He drove an old beat-up brown truck that could be spotted from far away.

I used to call him the Red Indian, not realizing that term was coated with controversy. Middle Easterners used that term for Native Americans to differentiate them from the people of India, the country that Christopher Columbus had supposedly thought his ship landed on. Figuring out what to call the Red Indian became a great topic of discussion, debates, and even confusion in my writers' groups. Some encouraged me to stay true to my word choice, which stems from and represents my culture. Others nudged me to consider replacing it with a less controversial word. I listened to what everyone had to say and shared it with the Red Indian. He responded, "Who gives a shit about that? If that's all I would have to worry about, I'd be happy. Some white people don't like to be called white. They want to be called Caucasian."

That's the short version of this conversation. The longer perspective is in another chapter.

I decided not to use "Red Indian" as it would remove the focus from the story for some people, but not all. I researched online to find words that felt right, like Goldilocks, who tasted the different bowls of soup placed before her on a table. I came across the Racial Slur Database, which had categories for 182 races. I toured the site, starting with Arabs, and discovered the following:

> Camel Crunch—From the cereal "Captain Crunch," only the Arabian version.
> Fadi—Common Arab name, the plural is Fadii (Fa-Die).
> Dusty Nuts—It comes from Arabs living in the desert.
> Firecracker—They blow themselves up.
> Habibi—Translates in Arabic to "Beloved". Technically a term of affection, but still sounds funny.
> Snigger—Short for Sand Nigger.
> Urban Turban—Arab who tries to act black.
> Terrorist—Self-explanatory.

Some expressions were comical, and others didn't make sense. How could habibi, beloved, and Fadi, a name, be slurs? I hopped from page to page through the different races and came across this description for whites—"bird shit" because bird shit is primarily white and "Betty Crocker" which referred to white women in general. For Italians, there was "garlic bread" with the caption "self-explanatory."

I scrolled through the countless terms, amused by the names people concocted to describe other races. How much work went into creating this database? I jumped off that site to do the research I was supposed to do on Native Americans. In the 1970s, the academic world felt that Native Americans was a more accurate and less stigmatizing word than Indians. They began promoting the term as a politically correct substitute for Indians. But this meant anyone born in the Americas, could be considered Native American, whether they were indigenous or not. So they felt "Indigenous people of the Americas" was the most accurate term. Yet because that term was too cumbersome for everyday speech, people stuck with Native Americans. Indians remained widely used.

Later, they recommended respecting one's identity by asking how they prefer to be called. But how does one make such a request for a book if everyone has different views? A site suggested that the most respectful way to address Native Americans is through their tribal affiliations. I did that, which led to the title "The Oneida Man."

The Oneida Man would walk into the video store, his thick, coarse hair as long as mine. Sometimes it flowed down to his waist, or he tied it in a hairband. Sometimes he walked in and out without saying a word. Sometimes he roamed in dead silence, approached the counter, and lingered around.

He waited to see if I would speak or not. Often, I was not willing. I had work or was on a phone gossip session with a sister or friend.

I found him peculiar, but yet, when he talked, he said intriguing things. Some things I jotted in my journal. Others I added later in my books, and others I turned into published poems. One such poem is *Love, Justice, and Turtle Soup*.

A Native American man with long hair walked into my place of business one day and verbally handed me a recipe, though I did not cook at the time—and now that I do cook, I doubt I could follow the instructions he gave though I'll never forget the recipe.

He said, nonchalantly, "If you want to make homemade turtle soup, you have to be careful and you must wait. You'd want to catch a sea turtle because you get thirty or more pounds of meat from it—depending on weight. You need help too. A couple of men would do, to place the turtle inside a garbage barrel filled with fresh water. Close the lid and leave it there to starve.

It sounds brutal, I know, but there's no other way to do it if you want to have homemade turtle soup. Sea turtles can live up to a hundred years, so dying takes a while. If someone tried to slaughter them, they'd release a poison into their system that would kill anyone who ate from it. One must therefore keep the area surrounding the garbage barrel quiet, so the turtle doesn't think it has been caught by anyone but itself...."

Turtles have a bad memory and will forget they were trapped.

People trap each other like that and call it love.

Elephants, on the other hand, don't forget. If someone tried to hurt them, they return in a hundred years to step on them.

People avenge each other like that and call it justice.

We didn't have your typical kind of conversation or friendship. We did not contact each other regularly or discuss our day's or life's happenings or struggles. In the beginning, I said nothing. I only listened. I tried to understand the purpose behind his presence. He often said things that stimulated my creativity and made me rethink history. To consider how our historical accounts—me as a Chaldean and he as a Native American—were related. He transferred basic ideas into unique and priceless treasures.

The Oneida Man was a matter-of-fact type of guy, a simple man living a meager existence. But then, gradually, he revealed himself as a profound person. Through these conversations, I saw his wisdom and willingness to admit to uncertainty. His humor, playfulness, wry character, and offbeat humor intrigued me.

Our friendship expanded to where he invited me to his niece's graduation. I met his mom. He once visited the home of my spiritual teacher, Chip, an elderly man who belonged to the Chippewa tribe. My older sister and I once invested in his brother's startup business. Not a sharp undertaking from our side (or his brother's), but nonetheless, we wanted their family to do well.

For various reasons, the Oneida Man and I lost contact for over a decade. I got married, had two children, and stayed home to raise them. When we reconnected, I began to write this book about our peculiar and even remarkable conversations. Our topics included Cleopatra's Dance of Darkness, our relationship with the Creator, and similarities between Chaldeans and Native Americans. Also, how he could die four times and be brought back to life four times.

CHAPTER 1

The Oneida Man

Ten years had passed since I'd last seen the Oneida Man. Then one afternoon in July 2014, I called the junkyard where I knew he worked to look for him. The answering machine came on with a woman's voice. I left a message, not knowing if he would ever receive it, if he had moved or was still alive. A few days later, while I was organizing my basement, a number from South Carolina appeared on my phone. It was him, the Oneida Man.

"You live in South Carolina now?" I asked.

"No, I'm still here. My sister lives there, and I got this phone while visiting her."

We exchanged niceties. His voice hadn't changed—soft, flat, and matter of fact. Minutes passed before I told him I was going through my journals and came across a conversation we once had two decades ago where he'd told me, "We want you to write about our stories." I did a little research but could not find stories like what he'd told me over the years about his tribe and other Native Americans.

"What you're going to find is a history that is favorable. It isn't a history that's truthful," he said. "It was not healthy to be a native a few hundred years ago. People were in hiding. They felt they were being hunted."

I told him I wanted to hear the stories I couldn't find in books.

"A friend of mine, who was eighty then, wanted to hear stories about natives. The people who he asked, the wise people, said to him, 'Me too.'" He laughed. "He died when he was ninety years old, but the old people said to him, 'Me too.'"

I told him how I sometimes feel the energy of Native Americans around me.

"The reason you feel that energy is because at Mound Road and M59 Highway, there were burial grounds for Native Americans. Now there are buildings, townhouses, and subdivisions. It's right on top of where the mounds are. That's why it's called Mound Road. That's just, for instance, native history to understand why you have certain feelings. Sterling Heights won't tell you where you are. They don't even know where you are."

I told him I wanted to learn more about his tribe and the areas where I've lived and worked since I came from Iraq to the United States almost thirty-five years ago. Who lived here, and how did they live? What happened to them? Who were Ryan, Dequindre, and Van Dyke, names given to the roads surrounding the city of Sterling Heights? He said I could visit the junkyard.

"It's a bit hard to find someone to watch my kids, so I'd have to bring them," I said.

"Oh sure, bring them. Do your kids like cats? I have eleven kittens that were just born."

"Okay, I'll bring them."

"*Nagewa*. That means 'see you again.' That's how we end a visit."

"*Nagewa*," I said, and we hung up.

The day I planned to see the Oneida Man, my sister-in-law called me on a sunny Sunday in August. She told me there were protests around the corner of my street about the violence against Christians in Iraq by ISIS (Islamic State of Iraq and Syria). They started at St. Mary's Assyrian Church at Fourteen Mile Road and went to Seventeen Mile Road where two protest groups met at that corner. Then they all walked back south toward Fourteen Mile Road. I dressed and met the rally as it came north toward our area. The kids were on their scooters, I walked.

"Where are we going?" my son kept asking.

I didn't know what to say. Do I tell him we are going to a rally, explain what a rally is and why it is taking place? He's five years old. Is he supposed to hear these things, and if not, when? How old does he have to be to hear the truth? Is it good to tell him the truth, or should he remain innocent? What about my daughter? She's eight years old. Should I explain to her that children are being decapitated in Iraq by vicious men, and we are out here to do what? Cry on their behalf? What good would that do the mother and father of the decapitated child?

The neighborhood was quiet, with only birds chirping and squirrels chasing each other. As soon as we stepped out of the subdivision onto Ryan Road's main road, we heard cars honking their horns and people shouting into megaphones. "Obama, Obama, where are you? Obama, Obama, shame on you! Christian Iraqis, they need you."

American, Iraqi, Chaldean, and Assyrian flags fluttered in the air like the leaves on a tree. Most protesters wore white T-shirts with the words "Stop Killing Iraqi Christians" in red. Others wore white T-shirts marked with a red N in Arabic, which stood for *Nasrani*. This letter was used by ISIS to mark the homes of Christians in the villages of Iraq. Signs and banners depicted pictures of murdered children and demanded that the US Government end the genocide in Iraq. "Obama, Obama, where are you?" shouted a protester leading the procession into a megaphone. The crowd followed his chorus. "Obama, Obama, shame on you! Iraqi Christians need you!" Later, we heard, "Down ISIS! Save Iraqi Christians!"

As we walked closer to the crowd, the powerful aroma of kabob grabbed our attention. Several Iraqi restaurants and produce markets stood on the corner of Seventeen Mile and Ryan Road. A large barbecue grill on the sidewalk offered protesters free hotdogs and cold bottled water. I asked who donated the food and drink, and they said, "The Ice Hookah and Tobacco Shop."

My children complained of the heat and fatigue. I assured them we would be home in five minutes, although I knew it would be longer. It was longer, closer to an hour. I had the chance to interview a few people and take down the name of the man holding the megaphone, Nabil Nona. He wore a red shirt and sunglasses and was probably in his mid to late thirties. On the way home, we came across two fruit trees, one growing red and the other green pears, which, as tradition had it, I ate from for nourishment during my afternoon walks. I plucked four green pears, poured a little water over them, rubbed them for cleanliness, gave one to each child, and kept two for myself.

Before turning onto our street, my son stopped at a house with a ceramic welcome sign planted in the grass and an American flag hanging from a large tree bark. He asked me to take a picture of him next to the flag. I didn't take him seriously since, for over a year, he had refused to take photos or, when forced to pose, refused to look at the camera. But when he insisted, I realized he was serious. Then I understood. He wanted to imitate the protesters who proudly raised their flags as I took their pictures.

Later that day, before taking the kids to Bible camp, we drove to the junkyard to visit the Oneida Man.

The junkyard was across the street from what once was our family's video store, which I managed for twelve years, and where the Oneida Man visited me to chat. It was now an Arabic produce market. The gas station on the corner of the road was once a pasture. Next door was a gravel pit, a hole filled with water. The place was called "Bare Ass Lake" by the kids who hung out there when they skipped school and drank beer all day. The ground is solid now. After years of being filled by the previous and current owners, it became a junkyard.

I parked the minivan. We got out, walked to the office, and I asked a man for the Oneida Man.

"He's inside; just go through the back."

"Mom, there are the kittens," my daughter said.

Eleven kittens sat beside the office porch. On the way, a woman walked out of the office and took a hard look at us. "You have new additions, I see," she said.

"Yeah." I realized that she was the Oneida Man's sister.

The junkyard was no longer a junkyard but filled with parked lorries and junk trucks. I could not see the Oneida Man anywhere. My kids were busy drinking the Slurpee and eating the snacks I bought for them from 7-Eleven, which now occupied what used to be my eldest brother's store. In a plaza he built, and over the years, it had various businesses, from a video store to a men's tailor shop, pizzeria, dry-cleaner, and mortgage and real estate office.

"Hi there."

I'd recognize that voice anywhere. He had talked to me often at the video store. A man with short hair appeared, holding a metal coffee cup. His body was the same, medium height, medium built, and although he wasn't very old, he had no teeth. But as long as I had known him, the Oneida Man had long hair, usually tied in a ponytail.

"You cut your hair," I said.

He sat on one of the two plastic chairs in front of a small trailer. He didn't comment about the hair and looking around, I said, "I've never been inside this place before."

"It used to be a junkyard, but now I lease it for these lorries to park in."

Several spider mosquitos landed on my shoulder. I shooed them away. My children played in the dirt as we talked. My son kept talking about poop and booty, and after some time passed, my daughter said, "Mom, I'm bored."

"Mom, you're bleeding," my son said, touching my shoulder.

There was a lot of blood.

"That's from the spider mosquito," said the Oneida Man.

I wiped the blood with my hands, and my skin turned pink. My children returned to playing, and I asked him to tell me about the mounds. I had read that Mound Road is named after an Indian burial ground, now destroyed, that was discovered near that road. It is believed that the earliest settlers of the Americas were in Michigan about twelve thousand years ago. The Europeans distinguished what they called "Mound Builders" from the natives they found because they assumed the Native Americans were too culturally uncivilized to develop such large and complex structures. Since the local natives failed to explain the origins of the mounds, the Europeans reasoned that their white race or advanced societies from the Middle East had once lived in the New World until the natives annihilated them.

The Oneida Man had a different take on this story.

"The reason the natives did not tell Europeans about the origins of the mounds was that, historically, we noticed that if you told the Europeans not to do something, they went ahead and did it just to see what would happen. That's their nature. So, we saw that it was better not to tell them anything because they belittled everything in America, going as far as raiding the ancient burial sites for treasures and artifacts."

Another observation the natives made was that the

Europeans always wanted to know why and how so they could change it. "They wanted to change everything instead of taking it as it is," he said. "They wanted to change everything because they viewed what they have as real and true and everything else that others had as unreal and fictitious."

In 1894, Cyrus Thompson of the Smithsonian Institution concluded that the Mound Builders were the Native Americans. Most of those who built those mounds had died of diseases or had been enslaved in the decades following the Spanish exploration of the region. The mounds were built over thousands of years by different people, ranging from hunter-gatherers to farmers. The earliest mounds in the United States were found at Watson Brake near Monroe, Louisiana, built in the late fourth millennium BC. Over a thousand mounds in Michigan have long since been flattened and turned into streets and lots.

"That's why there aren't many Indians here," the Oneida Man told me. "There used to be lots. Now there's no *lots*."

After the war with the British, cannons were set up in Detroit, Algonac, and Port Huron so natives who left for Canada could not return to their land. Treaties were made, at the point of a rifle, with various Indian tribes from 1814 to 1819, freeing up much land for settlement.

It was time to return home. On our way out, the Oneida Man pointed ahead and said, "There's a groundhog. You just missed him. We get rabbits here and deer, all kinds of animals. It's fun."

I told him we'd return one day, and we left.

CHAPTER 2

Holly Wood Makes Very Good Wands

The children off to bed but not asleep, I went into my office and lit a three-wick candle and an incense stick. I sat in front of my computer with a cup of coffee and called the Oneida Man. Three months had passed since I had visited him at the junkyard. The phone rang, followed by a clicking sound. "Hey there," he said. He never started a greeting with the word hello, perhaps because once he'd said "hello" is actually "Hell O."

I asked how he was doing.

"I'm good," he said in his flat voice that was low and, at times, difficult to hear. "I went and visited my grandkids in Canada. I try to go a few times a month."

"I went and visited my shaman," I said.

He laughed. "You did?"

"Yes."

"How was that?"

"It was fun."

During this visit, I met my teacher Lynn V. Andrews in person for the first time, along with my mentors. I was introduced to Lynn in the summer of 2011 through one of her books, *Writing Spirit*. I then called her for some literary advice, not knowing who she really was or what shamanism meant. Within six months, I found myself enrolled in her four-year school without walls which taught about mysticism and shamanism from the sacred feminine. These ancient teachings were passed down to Lynn from indigenous women from all over the world, particularly two Native Americans named Agnes Whistling Elk and Ruby Plenty Chiefs.

I finally learned what shamanism meant in the second year of school when I researched the word on Google. What I read surprised me. According to Wikipedia, shamanism is a religious practice that involves a practitioner (shaman) interacting with the spirit world through altered states of consciousness, such as trance. The goal of this is usually to direct spirits or spiritual energies into the physical world for the purpose of healing, divination, or to aid human beings in some other way. Reading this, I felt glad to have been oblivious to shamanism's meaning. Otherwise, I would have fled in the opposite direction.

I told the Oneida Man about the tools people had made and brought with them to the event, like drums and rattles. He told me how natives made drums and rattles. I then shared this with him. "I learned some natives boycotted my teacher Lynn's lecture a while back. I asked the mentors at her school why natives would do that, and they said that it was from past hurts. Natives don't trust people."

"That's true," he said. "Well, I don't trust you."

"Why? I wouldn't hurt you."

"I don't trust you wouldn't hurt yourself, so I have to protect you. You must be careful with knowledge because people fear the truth." He stopped, and I could hear him take a long puff of his cigarette. "The custodians, the American government, are custodians of this land and nothing more. They don't own it. They stole the ideology of this land and said it was theirs. That's why they get upset and treat you as if you are terrorizing the nation by telling the truth. Just because the government said Columbus found this place does not mean we were lost," he said. "Chris and his people came to the beach and did war measures. We had peace agreements with the queen and everyone, but they did not uphold their agreement."

He suggested I watch *The Elder Brothers Warning*, a movie that depicts the native side of colonization.

"First Nation people look at people that are not native, who call themselves shamans, and say, 'She is usurping the authority of someone that does it. She's a Beverly Hills Shaman.' That's where the apple comes from. No matter what she does, she has a silver spoon in one hand and a North American Shamanic title in the other hand. A Native Shaman does not have a silver spoon to begin with. Most people I know can't afford to cross the street, let alone get on the plane and travel worldwide."

"But if her teachings are helpful, then that's a good thing, isn't it?"

"Yes, but you don't have to chase it," he said. "It's in *you*. In other words, you didn't chase it. It came to you, so it's great for you to use the tools. All the teachings did was brighten things for *you* that were already in *you*. Other people who it's not in them, it takes a lot more to brighten it."

The nearby altar drew me into a little spell. It had a small gold elephant from India, a Tibetan Buddhist meditation bell, a Virgin Mary statuette, and family pictures. I thought of the women I had recently met. We each learned from the other on many different harmonic levels of consciousness, meanwhile not taking ourselves too seriously. I could not share this with the Oneida Man because of his doubts and criticisms, but I still moved along with our conversation, my heart open and willing to listen to his views.

"You understand more than if I was talking to Mrs. Andrews," he said. "She probably wouldn't get it or understand it as much as you do. Native Americans have a hard time with people who want something because they want it for themselves and not to help people. They do it for their portfolio. That's nice to have a Native American shamanic background in your portfolio, but it doesn't do the Creator any good. It's education, not spiritual. The Creator gives you something, a gift, and that's way more than using something to pound it over someone's head. With native people, they look at it like, 'Oh yeah, that's nice.'"

I listened, detached, knowing his mind was made up and honoring his viewpoint. It didn't lessen my love and respect for my teachers.

"Natives are like Iraqis; they've lost a lot," he went on. "Don't throw your pearls before swine. They've got everything already and are unhappy until they have everything else, even your living. And now they want to steal the Creator's gifts He gave you first. Then they'll tell you how to live after they learn it from *you*. That's how come the harsh feelings from the native people toward her."

THE ONEIDA MAN

My fingers danced across the keyboard as I typed. He waited for me to finish.

"Remember the white guy who did the sweat lodges, costing thousands of dollars?" he asked. "People came from all over, and three people died. Natives don't want that in their history. If you're not sick and you do a sweat lodge, you will be sick. It'll make you sick. These people come from Europe and do a sweat lodge, and they're not sick and die. That's the stupidest thing I've heard of. That's one extreme."

"Much of the criticism concerns her looks," I said, recalling the term "plastic shaman," which originated among Native Americans and First Nation activists to describe those falsely claiming to be shamans or traditional spiritual leaders without any genuine connection to the cultures they represent. Many of Lynn's critics focused on her appearance, given that she was a white, blonde woman from Beverly Hills who claimed to be a shaman. Some believed her claims were motivated by a desire for fame and fortune.

While critics warned of the risks of placing trust in individuals like Lynn, I believe there is always a risk in trusting any person or institution, whether a shaman, guru, celebrity, physician, academic, scientist, spouse, university, or religious temple. Ultimately, it is not the individual or institution that possesses power but rather the consciousness that animates that power.

"People are surprised when they see me because I don't look as native as they think I should," he said. "I look Scottish. People expect to see her as something else, and when they do, they're like 'Oh shit, that doesn't look like a shaman.'"

"I read somewhere that Hollywood misuses and abuses

the word shamanism," I said. "That's one of the reasons natives get angry about how others use the word."

"Natives had a very hard time with Hollywood. You know what Hollywood is? Holly wood is the stick from the holly tree, and Merlin was the king's magician in Europe. He would go around the country like a politician telling people what's good for them and why they should vote for him. Historically, a magician's wand was made of holly wood."

Upon researching Merlin, I discovered he is a figure from the Arthurian legend, a cycle of stories set in Britain in the Middle Ages. He was a wizard and a counselor to King Arthur and is often portrayed as having supernatural powers and knowledge. According to legend, Merlin was born of a mortal mother and an incubus (a type of demon), which gave him his magical abilities. He supposedly guided Arthur to greatness and played a key role in many of the king's adventures, including the quest for the Holy Grail. Merlin is also associated with the Lady of the Lake, who gives Arthur his famous sword Excalibur. Over time, Merlin became a popular figure in literature, art, and film, and has remained a beloved character in popular culture.

In addition, I researched holly wood and discovered that holly trees, sacred of Wicca and Witchcraft, make good wands that can banish unwanted entities and command evoked spirits. It is a favorite of ancient magicians. They used it in spells to gain success, take revenge, or achieve beauty, protection, luck, and dream magic.

"Magicians made people believe there was magic behind it all when it was an illusion," said the Oneida Man.

"Couldn't an illusion be the same as—reflect—reality?"

"If you want to believe that, yeah. It's like believing the sun comes up at six o'clock at night. It's not real. It's an illusion. If you believe it, it's real to you, but it's not real to nature. That's what an illusion is. It's a trick."

He coughed a deep cough that took a moment to clear up.

"People who call themselves shamans are, for natives, just an illusion, trying to pretend to be something that's not real," he continued. "On the other hand, some people can do a cause-and-effect on Earth. It's usually not personal. Of course, it's a prayer. You ask the Creator to do something, and the Creator responds. If people say they can do it themselves, they're probably a pretty big devil. It's one evil person trying to cause something for themselves or other people, and that's not good. When you ask something from the Creator, what you get might not be what you want, but it's the best thing for you. 'Oh Lord, I need patience, and I need it right now!'"

He laughed at the irony, and we were silent for a moment. I stared out the window into the dark sky and reflected on the common belief we shared; human beings are under a universal natural law, regardless of one's cultural or historical context. But I had mixed feelings about the topic of shamanism. There are no inherent reasons why a person of any race or ethnicity could not practice shamanism, as long as it's approached with respect, sensitivity, humility, and the willingness to deeply understand the traditional practices of the cultures from which shamanism originated. There are no reasons that they can't pass on those teachings. I am a living example of this.

Through my work with Lynn, I was able to overcome my

fears and complete a book, *The Great American Family*, which went on to win an Eric Hoffer Award. I also created a documentary with the same title, which has since earned over a dozen international film awards and is available on Amazon Prime. My journey with Lynn helped me rediscover the sacred feminine, which had been destroyed, buried, and forgotten in my birthland. I believe that the Great Spirit guided me to Lynn so that I could make this important discovery and share it with others.

If one believes in reincarnation, in being "born again," then one could have experienced being a person of white, red, black, or yellow in their past life; human races the Onedia Man introduced to me (I address this topic in another chapter). We simply don't know.

"I mentioned Hollywood, because that's the magician's wand, and it's not real," he went on, and I realized I'd missed part of what he'd said, my mind having wandered. "The whole Hollywood thing is not real, though they try to have you believe it's real."

"It's like that movie Captain Phillips," I said. "They made the captain a hero when, in reality, he jeopardized the lives of his crew. Even though the people on the ship came out and told the truth, no one did anything about the non-truth. The audience accepted the film as is."

"That's what I mean."

I had mixed feelings about this topic too. It's true that Hollywood is a highly commercialized industry, with a focus on profit and box office success. This often led to a lack of artistic integrity and an emphasis on formulaic, predictable content. Critics have argued that Hollywood has a negative influence on society, perpetuating harmful stereotypes and unrealistic expectations, particularly around body image and gender roles. Not to mention the violence and gore that infiltrates the screens, with action and horror films being popular film genres. During my twelve years managing the video store, I noticed most customers favored films that might be considered "junk food" for the psyche, with little or no concern for films that nourish the mind and soul.

But it's also true that watching movies can be therapeutic as well as entertaining and can offer insight into human behavior and history. They are a powerful medium for storytelling and can inspire us to reflect on our lives and make decisions on what we learn from them. They are gateways to different worlds. For the most part, that has been my experience.

"Some people relish the thought of shamanism," said the Oneida Man, drawing me away from my thoughts. Rain had started to fall by now. "Anyone with this much authority who can create the cause-and-effect of things is humble, and they wouldn't want you to think of them as magicians. They wouldn't call themselves shamans, to begin with. They would have a lot of experience because they care for many people, children and grandchildren and those who come to them with problems. They're normally wiser people. Generations of people make wise, not fifteen minutes of class."

He broke into another cough. A dog barked outside. The rain stopped as quickly as it had come.

"Ceremonies are nice, but some people will do it for every kind of reason. Some people do it just so people will listen to them, and it's not always good if you listen to them. They want to be a ringleader. It has nothing to do with the Creator. And then they have to lie and say, 'God told me to do this.' Well, when God tells me, I'll do it. Until then, you have fun."

"Don't you think ceremonies help move you toward your path?"

"Some ceremonies move you away from your path," he said. "You have to know, why are you doing this ceremony? What are you doing?"

"But it could be a good thing, couldn't it?"

"If you keep it simple, and it's a good ceremony with a good memory, your garden will grow. You'll get plenty to eat, to where you can share it with the neighbors. With a good ceremony, you'll get a lot of tomatoes. Get more than what you need." He chuckled. "Sometimes too much stuff is worse than not enough. Same with education. Some people want to stay unintelligent; they don't want to deal with it. They get into their little life and don't want to bring it further. Then some people are never happy with what they have and want more and more and more. And they throw out a lot of what they don't want. Some people are students their whole life, and they never use it. They store it."

A gentle breeze appeared outside, like a whisper. I glanced toward the motion and listened to the sound. Suddenly, I noticed my children's voices from afar. They were still not asleep.

"Some people don't need to do a ceremony for their garden because they always give thanks to the Creator," said the Oneida Man. "Ceremonies are about going back and forth and back and forth to the good side. People forget the good side, so they do have to do a ceremony to get back to it. They want to wander back and forth. That's like the children of Israel. They went back and forth, displeasing God, so He gave them commandments. And they gave it to everyone else, but no, I was not running back and forth, so I don't need commandments. I'm not that guy. I didn't wander back and forth in the desert for forty years. You did. I have ten thousand agreements, and you have Ten Commandments that you want me to remember every day, which remind me of bad things."

We remained quiet for some time, still. The wisp of smoke escaped from the long-burning candle flame and moved toward my direction, touching the waves of my long hair. I inhaled the sunlit mandarin berry fragrance and the patchouli incense. I fell into the rapture that occurs when the ego turns off long enough for a union with God to occur. I had nothing to say.

"My name and my spirit go further than I do," he said, clearing his throat. "And just because someone is old doesn't mean they're wise. Some portray elderly native people as very wise, blah, blah, blah, but to native people, a baby could be very wise. No one person is greater than another. Wise people make decisions considering the seven generations that are not born as opposed to what I need right now. I can make a decision for something I want right now, but it might not be a good thing for my grandchildren. A decision can be made by looking at the seven generations behind and the seven generations to come. It's harder to look into the future than it is to look at history. It's still a consideration for the future." He paused, then added, "You can take a magician class too."

"Are you offering any?"

He laughed. "Oh no! You never would know the outcome of that."

"You once said that things are changing, that people are becoming more aware."

"More people are waking up. That's what we call them. We can talk about current events. Since 1992, history has been changing. People are more concerned with smaller communities instead of federations. It was told that instead of being one world order, one guy telling the world what to do—how stupid!—most people are going toward communities with families. They are not following some fat cat telling you where to work and when to come home. They are becoming more conscientious of their neighborhood. The time for making a mess is over. People are unhappy with that, and they don't want it for themselves, their grandparents, their children, or their cousins."

There was a silence, and in it, I felt the heaviness of the night. The enchanting musical sound of the wooden wind chime knocked on my window. My eyes fell on the clock. The hour of sleep was once again past due.

"The wisest thing on this earth is common sense," he said. "People go to the moon when it's all there in front of you. They think if you pay a lot of money, then it's the best for you. If you do something and the community enjoys it, then it's a good thing. Whatever you do, the community has to enjoy it. Otherwise, it doesn't mean anything."

"Could they be looking for sovereignty?" I asked.

"Sovereignty?"

"Yes… well, do you think there is true sovereignty anywhere?"

"People don't govern themselves," he said. "People serve God. That's the problem with this country. The word sovereignty is a nasty word. It means to reign over. You're sovereign to your children right now, but when they come to age, then you should not be sovereign over them. Let them go and discover the Creator. They made the word sovereign sound good. They want you to say; I am sovereign over myself. As soon as you say that, you give up the Creator. I am not sovereign. I need help and other things."

"From God?"

"In the English word, God is dog spelled backward. Those who made the English language created that word, God. There is no God—for them. They are God, period. And they are serious. Every time you say God, you are referring to dog, which is manmade because there were no dogs in North America. They brought it with them. That's their God."

"What do you call it?" I asked.

"Manitu is what we call it, which means 'We can't say the name yet.' Manitu is in Georgian Bay. Michigan has two Manitu islands: the Great and the Good Spirit. We can't say the name yet. It's not his name because God might not be him. It might be her. Or it might not be her or him. God is God. Maybe we can say the name when we die. Christians, the first thing they say is 'Father!' Then they have a guy on a stick! How hokey is that? And then you have to look to the ground. The Creator is not in the ground."

"I remember you telling me once long ago about the word God being 'dog' spelled backward. I will research the roots of both words and your theory of how they're associated."

"You are looking for answers in their words, and you'll find their answers to these questions. 'Don't believe me. You watch and see.' That's what my father told me, and he was always right." Silence again, a bit of wind rose outside, then settled down before he restarted. "And you can write all this and say it's yours."

"No, I won't do that," I said with a peal of light laughter.

"No, do it. You can."

"No, I write memoirs, true stories, which I think are more fascinating than making things up."

He insisted, but again I declined and thanked him for his offer. The Oneida Man believes that everything belongs to the Creator, even words. Writers are composers of words, not creators of them, he'd once told me. He does not care to be quoted or to copyright his statements for fear they would be stolen. He gives them away for free because he doesn't feel they belonged to him in the first place. In ancient Mesopotamia, scribes didn't sign their name to their writing. So we don't know who wrote most of their stories. The Epic of Gilgamesh has many of the same themes and topics as the Hebrew Bible, especially the flood story, but we don't know who wrote it.

"The spirit of the air—that's why people make things up," he said. "There are people who were cast here and people who were lowered. Native people were lowered here by creation. Ishnaibai were lowered here to write, watch, and help those cast here so they don't hurt themselves. Some people make things up and are giddy about stupid shit that doesn't mean anything to anyone. Some are ninety years old, and they can easily act as though they are a seven-year-old child. You have to look out for those, especially when they have lots of money. They think they can buy anything, and they can. Then some people write serious, important things, and no one believes it."

His low and gentle voice became harder to hear as the night went further around the clock.

"Blacks talk about how badly they were persecuted, but hey, you're still here!" he said. "Not hardly too many natives are here. It's true that blacks had it bad, but they're still here, and that makes the difference." He paused, then quickly added, in a cheerier tone, "But anyway, you can write this and say it's yours."

I laughed. "No, I don't want to do that. I don't know any of this stuff. I like to share what I receive, and if it does any good, I did my job."

"You can write it and say you dreamt it or something," he said, laughing and teasing.

I began to suspect that he was alluding to a story in which a man had claimed that Lynn's experiences of the "Sacred Feminine" resulted from his masculine creative imagination, which he had shared with her during their time together. However, Lynn took legal action against him and ultimately prevailed in court, proving she had authored the books herself. The Oneida Man had evidently done an online search about Lynn. He knew only what others said about her.

"Well, I've had dreams, but not about these things. My dreams tell me what to do, who to talk to, and I follow."

He then said he had something for me. "I can show it to you, you can write about what's in it, but you can't have it because there isn't another one like it."

"I can't buy it?" I asked.

"I'm not a shaman. I'm not for sale." He chuckled. "You can't find it in the stars. It's for you."

"Okay."

"I've met you before."

"I know. You told me that before."

"I met you before."

"I know."

CHAPTER 3

Cleopatra's Dance of Darkness

The bookstore café was semi-full, and I sat amongst the other patrons at one of the tables. The Oneida Man, walking behind me, complied at first, but then, looking around, he said he preferred to sit in a more isolated corner. It felt like déjà vu. On the few occasions we met at the bookstore in the past, he always chose the most secluded areas. He did not want others to hear him speak.

As we settled in, he placed a book on the table and pointed at the cover. It was about Cleopatra. He brought out a set of old papers, unfolded them, and set them on the table.

"Cleopatra's dance of darkness," he said.

"What's that?"

"You won't find these stories in these books."

I waited for him to tell me about Cleopatra's dance of darkness, but instead, he talked about the moon landing. He said, "I don't think they ever went there. Many things fly around when you go that far, like rocks and junk. It's like driving in a sandstorm and not getting sand on your windshield. To fly in the universe and not get a rock punched through your tin can, that's silly."

He drank his coffee, and his smirk widened.

"The stuff that flips up there is like a bad tornado, and you drive through that, and you drive back?" he asked. "If you have a large telescope, you can see all that."

A few people passed by and headed to the magazines' area. He was quiet momentarily, then continued, "There's a whole belt around the earth with chunks of material as big as houses and cars. To go thousands of miles an hour and not hit anything—that's silly. They don't have enough rocket maneuvers to do that. So that's what I'm saying." He looked behind him on each side, then relaxed in his chair. "In an interview, one astronaut said he was the first man to pee on the moon. That doesn't even make sense. You went through all that to get to the moon, and that's what comes to mind?"

"Oh, I'm the first guy who peed in his pants!" he mimicked. "What kind of report is that? One from a first grader or kindergartener—not an astronaut. He meant that he went into a bag, but still. And that's just one thing."

More people passed by. He waited for them to disappear. I reflected on what I once read. Much of the conspiracy theories I'd read focused on the pictures the astronauts took. No blast crater beneath the six lunar landings where their powerful rocket engine had fired. No stars in the sky. The flag waved even though there was no air on the moon. Someone lost the original tapes recorded. And Buzz Aldrin, the first man to pee on the moon, said in one interview on *The Big Issue*, "If I could go back, I'd remind myself to turn on the camera as we left. I forgot, so we don't have any pictures of the lift-off from the moon."

There was a total of six manned missions that landed on

the Moon between 1969 and 1972. Over fifty years later, no progress has been made toward another manned landing on the moon or any planet. Once the barrier broke, why has it not been repeated or advanced?

"They raced with Russia and China," said the Oneida Man. "The whole thing was for satellite and weather communications so everyone can have a phone and Internet." He chuckled. "The fact that I said I don't think they went to the moon—I don't know for sure. But it's not feasible."

We drank our coffees during a moment of silence.

"So that's why I got onto this subject," he said. "They flag certain stories and make others up. They refuse to acknowledge that women had a higher hierarchy. Cleopatra lived in one of the last matriarch periods of that time. Cleopatra was a matriarch, and that's why the war happened. There were big wars at that time that people didn't know about, and Cleopatra won a couple of big wars. She kind of took over the Roman guy, Caesar. It was like she married him, not he married her. Everything is negative toward that woman, and everything is Caesar. But it was Cleopatra who ruled the Roman Empire at that time. That's why they burned Rome."

During ancient Egyptian society, the crown passed through the royal women, not men. The daughters of kings were all significant. Women were not only responsible for raising children, but they also worked. They owned and ran businesses and inherited property. They held high religious positions in the priesthood.

"They didn't write the history like that, that Cleopatra was the clan mother, that she won. They call her Caesar's wife and point to her femininity and promiscuity because she is female. They write about that because it takes away from all the positive things she did. They focus on her negativity to make her a negative person, but she took care of thousands of families and almost took over the Roman Empire. That's when the Roman Empire came after Cleopatra."

Schooled in science, politics, and diplomacy, Cleopatra could read and write the ancient Egyptian language. She came from a royal dynasty that had been ruling Egypt for centuries and was known for her intelligence, political savvy, and charisma. She also learned about the need to wed the cultures of both Greece and Egypt.

"Cleopatra was in the middle of the world, the middle of the clan system," he said. "When she married the guy from Rome, Caesar, she did that for a reason, but they took her power away. They suppressed the clan system to start what we know now as the judicial system."

A few more people headed toward the magazines section while others returned from there. The Oneida Man remained quiet, took a few sips of his coffee, and resumed. "They'd rather not have the clan system. They'd rather have the judicial system. The court system is the largest corporation in the United States. It's a form of tax, and it's operated on billions and billions of dollars."

"What's the difference between the clan and judicial systems?" I asked.

"If it's a clan system and you pass a red light, you say, 'Hey girl, give me the keys. You can't drive for two or three weeks. Your sister will drive you or you have to wait.' With the judicial system, you pay a big fine. Making a mistake is monetary with the judicial system."

He waited until I placed a dot in my journal and looked up at him after the last sentence.

"So, back to Cleopatra," he said. "Ancient people, her people, did the dark dance, where it gets cloudy for so long that there are no crops. She won a great battle by using the powers at hand. Her enemies had no food. People became sick and died from starvation with no sun coming from the cloud. The problem with the dark dance is that the enemies had nothing to eat, and neither did you. If you have a weapon and decide to use it against someone else, you have to be willing and able to take that medicine too. If you wish something on someone else, like your enemy, you should be able to take that on yourself without harm—or you die."

"Do unto others as you would have them do to you."

"Exactly. The dark dance is deadly to bring forth because it affects you and everyone around you. It throws everything out of balance, even the birds, fish, and other animals. Everyone loses."

The store clerk announced they were closing in ten minutes. I gathered my writing material, and the Oneida Man folded the old paper that he'd set on the table, the literature of which I had not had the chance to decipher.

"The patriarch society forced itself on the matriarch society," said the Oneida Man as we headed to the door, "but that does not mean that the matriarch society is not still there. It just means that it's not as prevalent. Everything that happened on the earth was because the Creator made it like this. There's a reason. It's not good or bad. If you look to the Creator, you will always find a reason why."

At home, I headed to my office after everyone went to bed. I researched Cleopatra's background and learned she was a member of the Ptolemaic dynasty during the Hellenistic period (323—31 BC). According to Timothy Doran, a professor of history, during the Hellenistic period, "The influence of royal ladies was big, as role models. And queens became benefactors of communities... with records of a profusion of temple building, private bequests, etc. by women."

I opened my Kindle and read Merlin Stone's *When God was a Woman*. She writes, "Most of the information and artifacts concerning the vast female religion, which flourished for thousands of years before the advent of Judaism, Christianity, and the Classical Age of Greece, have been dug out of the ground only to be reburied in obscure archaeological texts, carefully shelved away in the exclusively protected stacks of university and museum libraries. Quite a few of these were accessible only with the proof of university affiliation or university degree." Stone points out that women shared the psychological and social power of the Goddess. Dr. Margaret Murray from the University of London wrote that the true nature of the relationships involving Cleopatra, who had a rightful claim to the Egyptian throne, was misinterpreted due to a male bias.

I set aside the electronics for the night and curled up in bed imagining Cleopatra doing her mystical dance, spinning around like the whirling dervishes of the Sufi tradition, the ecstatic dances of the Shakers, and other indigenous dances performed in cultures around the world. As the music began to play, her slender figure that was adorned with an elaborate dress and jewels started to sway rhythmically. Her loose hair curls swayed with her. Her feet tapped the Earth and her arms extended gracefully. Her movements were fluid and graceful as she glided across the dance floor. She was completely lost in the music, her body moving almost instinctively in response to the beat.

The tempo of the music increased. Her ladies who circled around with drums, tambourines, and rattles began to chant. Cleopatra became more energetic and dynamic, her great beauty exemplified. She twirled around with abandon, her body seemed to defy gravity as she moved effortlessly through the air and reached deeper and deeper into the spiritual realm. Her face was alive with emotion, her eyes closed in concentration, her long neck stretching in four directions: south, west, north, and east. Her olive skin tone radiated under the moonlight. She even captivated the stars with her presence.

As the dance came to a close, Cleopatra slowed her movements, gradually bringing her body to a gentle stop. She took a deep breath, her chest rising and falling with excitement and exertion, before finally opening her eyes and looking out at her ladies with a look of satisfaction.

CHAPTER 4

At the Junkyard

"Well, grab a chair," said the Oneida Man. He appeared from behind several small trailers. After he spoke, he turned around and disappeared.

I followed him, walking over dirt and pebbles in my high-wedged sandals. We arrived at a courtyard partly enclosed by trucks and trailers. I set my keys, iPhone, notebook, pen, and the cup of hot chocolate I'd bought from the corner gas station on the high table made of thick lumber. Then I grabbed one of the four white plastic chairs and sat down.

The Oneida Man told me he's remodeling his micro home. He'd built it in the shape of a trailer suitable for a maximum capacity of one person.

"How long will it take you to finish?" I asked.

"My whole lifetime," he said, crossing his legs and lighting a cigarette. Beside him was a table made of lumber like the one beside me. On top of it was a large mug, a pack of cigarettes, and a lighter. "I work slow."

The tree branches that hovered over us fanned the July heat away, creating a soft and cool breeze. The sun shrunk in the sky, behind the giant trees, resembling a yellow peach.

"What kind of trees are these?"

"That's a Chinese elm," he said, pointing to my right. He pointed to the left. "That's twisted sister." He laughed. "I call her that because she's twisted. It's actually a willow tree."

"It's so hot, I was hesitant to buy a cup of hot chocolate, but these trees create the perfect weather for it."

"Some people come here and don't want to leave because it's peaceful. I keep it peaceful. Some people don't even recognize it's peaceful. They want to be here. They're not in a hurry to leave. It's nice here, but I'm ready to let that go. It'll be peaceful wherever I go."

There was a moment of silence.

"When did you cut your hair?" I asked.

"A few years ago."

"You cut it little by little or all at once?"

He scissored his hands. "Chopped it off—one time."

"For as long as I'd known you, your hair was as long as mine."

"Since I was ten, I had long hair."

"Why did you cut it?"

"Because I was hot. It was summer, and I cut it."

I remained quiet.

"Said, 'I'm done with all this.' I went beyond it. I'm not even native no more. I'm my Creator's person. Native is for young people. All the native bells and whistles don't mean much no more. I used to help natives before with their issues. I moved on. It's not important anymore. I have other things I'm doing now." He puffed his cigarette. "Native is like… I think I told you before on the phone. The clan system helps you develop as a person and native person. It brought me so far, but it restricted me from my growth with the Creator. And I think this. I'm not really sure."

"I feel that happening to me," I said. "Before, I identified myself as an Iraqi and addressed and wrote about my peoples' issues, but I'm becoming less of that...."

"But you're not becoming American—just more personal."

"A person," I clarified.

"There are people who can't set their titles, history, and customs down. I don't need all that."

"Were you born in Canada?"

"Yes."

"So you're Canadian?"

"I'm North American."

I frowned. "Is there such a thing, or are you joking?"

"I'm serious."

"It says that on your passport?"

"Yup. Didn't I show you before?"

"No."

He reached for his back pocket and brought out his wallet. He opened it, and as he tried to get his passport card, wiped the plastic and chuckled. "Have to remove all these cobwebs."

He handed me the card, and I read it. It identified him with his tribe.

"Not all natives have this card," he said.

"Why do you?"

"Because we made an agreement with the British that they can be here. We didn't have war with them, play war with them, or kill each other. We made agreements which were policies. That gives some natives, not all, this North American citizenship. Some natives wanted to fight."

"What happened to the ones who wanted to fight?"

"They were probably beaten, and they became good American citizens." He laughed. "You're afraid of that leaf?"

I'd looked over my shoulder several times. I heard a noise of something fluttering nearby.

"It keeps dancing around you," he said, smiling. "It likes you."

The rustling continued and then appeared a brown and crunchy leaf.

"Do you consider yourself Christian?" I asked randomly.

"Oh yeah, I was baptized six times."

I laughed, and so did he.

"I must have been a real bad guy," he said. "It doesn't hurt to get baptized."

"Six times?"

"Once when I was born. Once when I was older. Once a friend wanted to get baptized and asked me to get baptized with him. Once, my wife wanted to get baptized and asked me to get baptized with her. Another time another friend wanted to get baptized and asked me to get baptized with him." He smoked his cigarette. "One friend told me, 'Yeah, but you didn't get baptized in the spirit.' I said, 'You were there? How would you know? I can't say what your spirit is. I'm not God.'"

"Why did he say that to you?"

"Because he was baptized in the spirit." Then imitating his friend, "' You weren't baptized in the spirit.' Ah, I think I was. For someone to say you weren't baptized in the spirit is very negative. I wouldn't say that to them. I'd say, 'That's good. Now you can start living like that any time.'"

A black cat with white fur around its stomach walked out from under the truck parked in front of me.

"Does she come here often?" I asked.

"Yeah, there are three of them that come here."

I made note of this and said, "You died six times; you were baptized six times."

"I died four times."

"Baptized six times. Maybe that's the trick."

"Yeah, maybe. I died four times. The doctors told me that. Actually, the Federal Marshall because I'm a citizen of North America. I'm in the hospital bed, I wake up, and he says, 'You died.' And I said, 'If I'm dead, so are you.' He said, 'Oh no, we're alive, and so are you.' Then I thought, what does that mean, I died, and now I'm here? What does that mean?" The cigarette smoke swirled in the air, nearly touching the tree branches. "I was poisoned, and it makes you very drunk. I don't have any memory of it."

We sat quietly.

"Thanks to the Creator, I'm here. Not harmed."

"Maybe you did something good in your past life."

He smiled. "Maybe."

"Do natives believe in reincarnation?" I asked.

"Everyone is different, and I've learned that different people think differently, regardless of their group. Many believe you're here to learn certain things to prepare for the spirit world. The Creator gives you the will to live, and you don't harm yourself because you're afraid of the unknown. Maybe if you knew it's better out there, you might leave early."

"What's that sound?"

"It's a love dove," he said.

"I hear it often in the morning, and I know the word for it in Arabic but not in English. I'm usually alone when I hear it and have no one to ask what bird makes that sound. It reminds me of my birth country."

"Doves nest on the gravel, and their eggs look like pebbles," he said. "They go and make sounds so you don't chase them and get away from their nest. Doves represent peace because of the story of Noah's Ark. Noah first sent a raven to see if there was land, and the raven didn't come back, so it was considered a bad bird. He then sent out a dove, and the dove returned with an olive leaf, so it was considered a good bird."

I looked around. "Do you make your food here?"

"Yes, I have a refrigerator and a stove. Do you want a sandwich?"

"No. I don't see any kitchen items. I thought you bought meals ready-made."

"Oh, I cook. I had spaghetti earlier today. Do you want me to make you a sandwich?"

"No, no. Just wondered how you prepare your food."

"I have everything in there, even a TV." He got up. "I want to show you something."

He went into his trailer and returned with a large map. He opened it on the table and pointed to Niagara Falls. "The Falls were here, and they moved here. They are moving inches a year and have washed out that much." He showed me by placing a distance between his hands.

Niagara Falls has moved back seven miles in 12,500 years and may be the fastest-moving waterfall in the world.

"Some people say, remember when the Falls were at the bay? That's when dinosaurs were here, ten, fifteen, twenty million years ago."

"Is that true?" I asked.

"No, it's a joke. Like you know the Dead Sea?"

"Yes."

"I remember when it was sick."

It took a while to get what he meant.

"Do you know French?" he asked, closing the map and entering the other trailer.

"I took four years of French in college but learned very little."

"Do you have a friend who knows French?"

"Yes, one of my friends translates French."

"I have something for you." He looked into a few corners. "I have it here. I'll find it."

"Where's the garbage?" I asked. He answered something, and my eyes found a green garbage can in the corner. I threw out my empty cup and, walking back, I watched my orange-painted toenails above the pebbles and dirt. Scattered between the pebbles and dirt were about six razor blades. Otherwise, the area was clean.

He came out with a stack of large papers that had turned yellow from old age.

"These writings might be before the United States," he

said. "The French and Dutch were here trading before the English. New York used to be called New Holland, and New York City was New Amsterdam." He set the papers on the table. "These are very old papers about the French relations to a group of people and how they related to one another and made agreements. You can't find papers like this except in the Smithsonian. You can keep them. I don't know what they say, so you can tell me after translating it."

I placed them beneath my notebook.

"The Native Americans here came from the south," he said. "They followed the ice. As the ice melted, people moved to its edge." He returned to his trailer and brought a Michigan map. "That's why too, there's Algonquin Park. It means people that walked the ice. Algonquin people entail all of us because we lived in central America and Mexico, and we all followed the ice to the south. It was a violent ice storm. Winds can carry you away for hundreds of miles and you'd be dead. You couldn't live there. There's nothing you can do."

I began to walk toward my car. He was several steps ahead of me.

"Before the ice age, there wasn't really a history," he said. "It wasn't lost but it's unnecessary to bring it up."

A car with a man and woman in it drove into the junkyard.

"That's my sister," he said. "She comes in to check on the place."

We arrived at my car and stood there. I noticed the empty cups on the floor near the fence. "So, what do you think about Christianity?" I asked.

"If people lived as Christians, it would be a different world," he said. "Jesus was here."

"Here where?"

"In North America. Jesus didn't just walk the Mediterranean. When he rose, if that's what people say, didn't he say he would talk to all the people in the world? I believe he came here because people had very strong feelings toward Christianity. It wasn't new to them. The heathens already know about it, not necessarily Christianity but the spirit of Jesus. This isn't the end of things but the beginning."

CHAPTER 5

Dying, Again and Again

"Remember once you told me you had died?" I asked the Oneida Man over the phone.

"Pardon me?"

"You said that you died?"

"I died lots of times."

"The time when the doctors resuscitated you," I said.

"I died four times that time," he said, then coughed.

"How can you keep dying at the same time?"

"I died, and they brought me back, I died, and they brought me back, I died, and they brought me back, I died, and they brought me back. I was poisoned."

"How long were you gone for?"

"I don't know. I traveled, though."

"How do you feel about it?"

He coughed for a little while. "I feel good about it."

"Was it a nice trip?"

"No, I'm just no longer afraid of dying. I do what I'm supposed to do, and one thing I'm supposed to do is talk to you."

A moment of silence inched itself into our conversation. I was sitting in my home office. The clock on the living room wall tick-tocked. A faint sound came from my son's bedroom as he played video games. The vanilla-scented candle flickered in the dark room. So did the computer and moonlight coming through the window. The smoke danced upward from the incense stick and zigzagged left and right like a belly dancer.

"You were attacked, weren't you?" I asked, breaking the silence.

"I was attacked and poisoned," he said. "That's why I cough the way I do. I was supposed to swallow the poison, but I didn't swallow it; I breathed it. The doctor said if I had swallowed it, I would have been dead. It was only in my lungs and then my blood. Had it gone into my stomach, that wouldn't have been good. I was in the hospital for over a month, intubated."

"Were you in pain?"

"I don't know what pain is," he said earnestly, then laughed. "No, they had me out and drained my lungs."

"Was it a near death or a death?" I asked.

"I'm trying to find the right word." He paused. "I'm drawing a blank. I don't know how to talk about that. Because of the things I was doing for other people at the time, there was so much negativity and groups against me. I don't know which group got close enough to do that."

"Were they natives or non-natives?"

"Native and non-Natives." He laughed, lightly. "It's like a dream. When you're dead, it's like a dream. There's a dream state where there's no feeling and it doesn't matter what people did or what happened. It's not fear, shock, love or hate. I can tell you what it isn't, but I can't tell you what it is. But I did travel. I wasn't in one place. I was in a thousand places with a lot of different entities—wasn't animals, monsters, people, ants—it was awareness. I traveled through a lot of awareness. It wasn't any one place. I was intubated for ten dates, and they did nothing."

"What do you mean?"

"The doctor said he did nothing. He said you died four times, and I didn't do anything to bring you back. I said then why do you want $250,000? Cause the bill was over $250,000. He was flabbergasted. I healed myself or the healing came. I don't know the cause and effect of it."

"You feel that totally changed you?"

"No. It didn't change anything. I mean myself personally. It might have changed everyone around me—doctors, nurses, and anyone who knew anything about it. Maybe that's what the Creator used me for. The doctors were amazed that I came out of it. Basically, I shouldn't have survived or should've been a vegetable. It flipped them right out. Maybe the Creator used me to show them things happen whether you want them to or not. After two weeks, I was out and about and that's when I came to the store and met you."

"Where?"

"At the video store twenty years ago. That's when we started talking."

"What did you say?" I asked.

"I apologized to you."

"For what?"

"For using you. I had a poor marriage, and I had a girlfriend who was very poor to me and I didn't want a girlfriend but I wanted a friend and I used you as a friend. You helped me transition from needing a girlfriend to needing a friend. So, you helped me."

We were both silent. I assumed he meant he apologized in silence, because based on my memory and journals, this conversation never verbally took place.

"There are several ways to create cause and effect around you," he said. "I wouldn't suggest dying four times to do that. I wouldn't suggest that. It wasn't up to me."

"So, how do you know you're supposed to talk to me?" I asked.

"I don't."

"You just said you did."

"I said maybe." He chuckled, knowing that was not true. "I just like you as a person."

"Well, I'm supposed to talk to you."

I asked him if he knew why natives were attracted to me. Over the years, they often came to my door and eventually became my teachers. I never pursued them, but there was a connection when they appeared. He said, "There are four types of people on this earth—blacks, red, whites, and yellow. In the last two hundred years, especially after World War II, races intermingled, resulting in interracial families. Do you consider yourself black?"

"No."

"You're not black, and you're not Asian. You don't live like white people, so you're native," he said. "People in the Mediterranean region are also natives. Your whole background and that of your family is native. You like to say you're Iraqi, and that's good, but you're not white, black, or yellow. If the

Mediterranean people were not messed with as much as they were, your history would be closer to American Natives. Your DNA is closer to Native Americans than all these other groups. You think you're meeting American Natives, but you're native."

Wrapping the orange and red patchwork quilt around my arms, I listened.

"The earth was all one place before," he said. "There was no ocean separating the world. If you googled the earth before and squashed the continents together, it made one continent. The continents drifted apart over the years, but there are still the plates of the earth. We live in Michigan now, and your family was born and raised in the Mediterranean. If the land was one big piece, you were only 6000 miles away from here. You can say that God sent us here or whatever they call God, the Creator. Or we were put here. And it's a great thing to be born here and live here. It's your turn. People don't see it as a great thing, but it is. It's your turn."

"Most Iraqis don't have the connection—that we're native," I said.

"They forget it over so much time. Like Iraqis and Iranians, they're the same people, but they hate each other so much. If you don't have people instigating two groups, they probably don't hate each other so much. Some people can do that with your family too. 'Oh, you know what they said about you?' That's what Europeans do. They want what you have for real cheap, making you a despicable person. You have to remember that the people in Iraq were taught English for a hundred years. That's a long time. A lot of Iraq's history was given to them by England and now, of course, by the United States. And the same thing in Iran and the same thing with Jordan and a lot of those countries. Some of those countries have their own history but a lot of it was given by Europe."

"Then why am I remembering?" I asked, referring to ancient history.

"Because you already answered that when you said you want to help people through your writing."

"I heard that Iroquois were once violent against their neighboring tribes and then against the settlers."

"Iroquois were not violent. They were strict. We were trying to meet the white people when they came here. We knew they were killers because we watched them for thousands of years when they were in Europe. We knew the way they did things was very brutal. Iroquois, it was their job to meet the people when they came here, and when they came, we had to be strict. They put that title on us, from strict to violent. That's what the Europeans said. Just because we said 'no,' they called us violent. We treated these people like children. Most were convicts who knew how to kill and steal and should have been left in Europe. The worst of Europe came here."

I drank my coffee, now cold, and continued to listen.

"When you stood up as a real native, the goal of the people who came here and are in power today is to denounce you. Make you a smaller person than you are. They do that through all manners of things. They persecute your person and go after your credibility before they even know you. They use the word violent because it suits them. You have to realize who wrote the books and the history. We didn't name-call, we didn't change words. They use the English language to change your thoughts. I can talk to them, and they would write it in English, and it's not what I said. That's why native people have a hard time with people talking for them."

After a short silence, he said, "There's a lot of negativities out there, so I don't understand why that lady from Hollywood would even want that."

He was referring to Lynn V. Andrews. I said, "It seems that the biggest difference between matriarchal and patriarchal communities is that, where women rule, there was and is no need for so much violence."

"Possibly, but then again, nothing is more fierce and violent than a mother defending her children," he said, amused. "We have a so-called patriarchal system based on control, ownership, commodities, dominances, and power hierarchies. But I do not believe we need a matriarchal system. We need something new."

"I agree, a system that is not based on either sex but on collaboration, cooperation, and inclusiveness centered around the family group. Where both males and females have equal power and roles. This might've been the natural system for most human development and is still the natural system, like the Kogi people."

I watched the documentary *From the Heart of the World: The Elder Brothers' Warning*. It introduced the Kogi (Jaguar) people, the "Elder Brothers" of humanity, who live hidden in northern Columbia in what they called "The Heart of the World." They revealed themselves in the early 1990s to warn us of the calamity we are creating. They call us children who do not know how to take care of the world.

Kogis wear all-white clothing but are barefoot because shoes would break contact between the people and the earth. They base their lifestyles on their belief in "Aluna" or "The Great Mother," the force behind nature that talks and teaches right from wrong. They ask people to stop digging and digging and taking out the mother's heart, cutting out her liver, heart, eyes, mouth, and ears. "The Mother is sad," one elder said, "and the world will end if we don't stop digging and digging."

It was sad how, for decades, outsiders have stolen the indigenous people's land, culture, and language, even stealing their spirits. But this pattern was not reserved to relationships between Native Americans and Westerners. The indigenous people of ancient Mesopotamia have been least protected. Their culture and language were most violated, and their stories and history are most stolen from outsiders and insiders, Easterners and Westerners. None of their violators have offered the sort of retributions other groups who experienced suffering or genocide have been given.

Like the Kogi, the civilization that built ancient Mesopotamia, the cradle of civilization, was sophisticated. They were more aligned with life and consciousness with who they are as Spirit. The Kogi had members of their societies called Mamos, which means sun, for guidance, healing, and leadership. They are like tribal priests. According to an online platform, the Temple of Theola, the first shamans appeared in the Tigris, Mesopotamia area. These people evolved separately from the other two main species of humans. In old accounts by the other humanoids, they were called the Gods, the Giants, the Watchers, and the Nephilim. They were actually Neanderthals.

The article states that "These Shamans had a dream culture which was when spirituality was first discovered."

I moved on to the next subject, the wheel, which Sumerians invented in ancient Mesopotamia to make work easier. I asked him about the significance of the wheel to Native Americans and why they built things in circles while the rest of the world built squares.

"Nature is round," he said. "Eggs are round. Your head is round. Square is manmade. If you look up anything with Tics, like mathematics, lunatic, politics, plastic, diabetic, it's the study of all kinds of shit that doesn't make any sense because it's not nature."

He started to talk about nature.

"When you talk to the flowers, you exhale," he said. "Flowers need carbon dioxide. It's healthy for them. When you breathe on the flowers, they're saying, 'Why don't you give me more carbon dioxide? Why don't you cough?' Because they're relying on your carbon dioxide, and you're relying on their carbon monoxide."

He brought up mosquitos, asking, "You know how mosquitos find you? You think they happen to find you. They come from half a mile away and follow your breath to your face because it's carbon dioxide, and then they'll land on you and bite you for your blood."

He moved on to the subject of trees.

"The people that came here cut all the trees because we were using it for medicine," he said. "The trees you see here were planted about two hundred years ago. None are the original trees. They did not want you to remedy and heal yourself but to need their doctors and hospitals." He was quiet momentarily, then added, "I'm being radical one way, but it's the opposite of their being radical the other way."

He said that some natives before they make their drums, talk to the tree to give up their pieces for making things like drums and pipes. By talking to the trees, one makes the wood come alive. "We make our drums out of cedar and make thirteen sides, and you stretch it with elk or deer hide."

"What do the thirteen sides represent?" I asked.

"It represents thirteen moons of the year," he said. "We have thirteen seasons because we work with the moon. Females also have thirteen cycles in the year. This is how we do things in the Great Lakes. Other tribes do things differently. We don't fight about how you do something. Everyone washes their faces, but everyone does it differently. Whatever you learn is great, but you have to remember there are many different ways to do things. Like in your area, they want peace and prosperity from the Creator, and they do that by enjoying what they do." He paused and then continued, "So anyway, if you talk to a cedar tree when you make it, you have a live drum. I had a drum but gave it to a young man."

"Why did you give your drum away?"

"I was interested in him doing well. He just graduated high school and couldn't find his way, so I gave him my drum so he would not go partying and smoke weed."

"You once told me that you're the wolf clan. What did you mean by that?"

"There are a lot of different clans, like groups of families that do things in memory of certain entities. Clans of the species with talons, like hawks and eagles, live their lives giving reference to the animal they represent. We have clans of species that have become extinct since the white people came here. They are not wolves, dogs, or raccoons. There are no words to describe them in English. Still, families remember them. It's remembering this animal while preparing food, eating dinner, or even washing. Natives know they're not on this planet alone and need everything around them to have balance. They know that the animals, plants, flowers, and trees are just as important as we are because the Creator created them."

I asked if he knew what a power animal was, and he said he did not. No one taught him that before.

"I am the wolf clan," he said. "There's the turtle clan. They are more home-based. The bear clan is about giving medicine to people from plants and animals. The wolf clan is about hunting food, gathering information, and bringing it to the people. It's about how you live your life. It's the symbol of your clan. It's a spiritual thing. I'm not out at night, like a wolf, looking for caribou," he snickered. "Wolves are very affectionate. They have yellow eyes. They hear your heartbeat from twenty feet away, they become apprehensive, you become apprehensive, and they want to see what you are. You don't want them near. And it goes back and forth like that. Same as dogs."

"What does a wolf represent for you?"

"We just say wolf. It's an identity, the essence. It's the spirituality of it, not the physical. And people don't understand that, and they befriend wolves and get eaten up because that's what wolves do. People are physical. Everything to them is physical, not spiritual. They have to learn spirituality. Children are physical. That's why they strike out. What you've seen is the spiritual side of it, not the physical. Once you see that, sometimes it's humorous, sometimes it's scary. It's still an entity that's good instead of getting a riffle and shooting wolves. If you claim a clan, then you're claiming that spirituality."

I had read somewhere that the animals were not the spirit but that the spirit assumed the shape of the animal and the attributes thereof. A spirit that materialized as a beaver was like God, appearing as a burning bush to Moses. Some natives believe that each individual is connected with an animal guide that offers power and wisdom to the individual when they communicate with it, conveying their respect and trust. This does not necessarily mean you pet or spend time with this animal, but more that you are open to learning its lessons.

The Manataka American Indian Council stated on its website, which has since been suspended, that "Animals do communicate with man by receiving mental messages, and they carry this ability with them in Spirit as they die. Communicating with animal spirit guides is not easy. Some messages from them may be confusing, if not impossible to understand, without considerable practice and patience."

"You once told me that the people of the Earth had a clan at one time."

"In Scotland, one of the biggest clans was the Thistle Clan," he said. "Today, most people of Scotland do not consider plants because the kings and queens took away the value of this memory with alcohol. They used alcohol to dumb down people. That's why, when Europeans came here, we thought they were dumb. Where's the beer barrel or by golly, I'll shoot your head off!" he imitated. "Today, the situation is the same with natives."

Today was a full moon, so I asked him, "What's the difference between a new moon and a full moon?"

"They're the same thing," he said. "They're both full. It's just that you have to see the new moon in the daytime because it's full. You can't see it at night because it's on the other side of the earth. You see the full moon at night. The moons were used to decide the best time to plant something. On a full moon, you plant things in the ground, like potatoes, because the seeds do better. You plant things above the ground on the new moon, like cherries. Much is controlled by the moon, like fishing, hunting, planting, and the seasons. I say controlled because you cannot do it, but it affects everything, including animals, especially wild animals.

"Because of religion and how people are taught, it affects people differently. On a full moon night, the police say they're busy and have difficulty dealing with people. People are drinking, and there's a lot of crime. It's not because that's the natural way of responding, but they've been taught that way. There are a thousand things that people are raised on that make them behave poorly. The effect is not as bad in countries other than the United States. If you go in the Pacific Rim Islands, if they have not been taught about monsters and goblins when they were little, then they can be very relaxed and enjoy the full moon as a gift from God and not, 'Oh, I have to behave like an asshole because it's a full moon.'"

"According to the books, Jesus was the son of God and not the sun in the sky. His clan would have been his Father. He went above all the clans on earth and went to the Father. His awareness was with his Father, so they killed him. He went by the awareness of the wolves, so he's not the wolf. He went by the awareness of the eagle, so he's not the eagle. He put himself above all the clans and all the people."

"I'm not sure I understand," I said.

"Mommy, can I have three birthdays?" my son asked, surprising me. It was after eleven o'clock at night, and I thought he was already asleep. I told him I'd talk to him about that later, and he walked out of my office.

"Everything we do in our lifetime is to learn about God," said the Oneida Man. "Everything is an avenue to the Creator. The wolf entity is almost benign to me. It doesn't matter. Your family doesn't mean much as you get older because your relationship is with the Creator. Say your mother right now; she can't worry about you as much as when she was healthy and you were young. She's not worried about you anymore. She worries about where she's going and who she will see when she arrives. I'm getting to the point where I understand what the Creator wants more than my family. Right now, your concerns are for your mother and your children and to take care of them. But you'll get to the age when the wolf is like everything around you. As you get older, you let everything go because all that takes care of itself. I do things that correspond to my Creator. It's a growing thing. I'm not saying I'm as far along as other people are. I'm saying I'm letting my family go. What's important is where I'm going."

It was getting late, so we said our goodbyes, and after hanging up, I did not go to sleep. I kept thinking of the wolf, who happened to be Lynn's power animal and mine, or so I discovered when I was in the shamanic school. I wrote about this experience in my four-part memoir series.* I never shared this information with the Oneida Man, but I wondered if the wolf was part of what connected us too, as well as, perhaps, a past life.

* *Healing Wisdom for a Wounded World: My Life-Changing Journey Through a Shamanic School*

CHAPTER 6

Sleeping Bear Dunes

I enjoyed walking Teddy in the warm weather in early May and watching King Charles crowned on television, not in real life. Many didn't like seeing Camilla crowned. They raved on social media that Princess Diana was their forever real queen. Others advised to move on. Diana is dead; even if alive, she could not be queen as she divorced Charles. They pointed out that, for all her status, Diana remained insecure. Her desire to do good for others resulted from deep feelings of unworthiness. Thus, the need for attention. The Oneida Man thought it ironic that her name was "Princess Di*e*."

I packed my laptop and headed to the coffee shop to write the chapter on Sleeping Bear Dunes. Sleeping Bear Dunes is a park in Michigan named after a Chippewa legend of the sleeping bear. According to legend, an enormous forest fire drove a mother bear and her two cubs into the lake for shelter to reach the opposite shore. After swimming many miles, the two cubs waded behind and eventually drowned. The mother bear arrived on shore and waited for her cubs to appear.

"That's a touching and nice story," said the Oneida Man when I told it to him after returning from a family trip to

Traverse City. There, we visited the Sleeping Bear Dunes. "A lot of tourist places have a mythical story, which is the attraction."

"The Great Spirit created two islands," I said, reading off the Internet. "North and South Manitou Islands to commemorate the cubs. The winds buried the sleeping bear under the sands of the dunes, where she waits to this day."

"That doesn't sound like a gift from the Great Spirit," he said. "It sounds like a mother that couldn't care for her cubs."

The young server placed an antique copper tray on my table. A matching coffee kettle, Turkish coffee cups, a sugar container, and a small spoon were on it. I removed the lid from the kettle and poured the first shot. I returned the top to the kettle. It fell off and made a banging sound on the tray. I again placed it on the kettle, and then returned to the notes to connect to the spirit of the story.

He said the Manitou in Canada originally came from the Michigan region, Manitou Island, meaning "the Creator's Island." When the English and the Americans fought during the Revolution and other wars, most Indians didn't want to join either side. So they went to Manitou Island in Ontario to escape the fighting.

"It was not a real war, but a war on paper to set a border," he said. "In their mind, you can't have a country unless you have a border, so there could be policing and taxing, etcetera."

The lid slipped off the kettle and fell on the tray, making a loud noise and startling me. I returned it to its place and suddenly the wilderness of Manitoba, Canada, came to mind. It's the setting for several of Lynn's books, where her teachers supposedly lived. Lynn claimed that she had changed the names and locations of her autobiographical accounts for the protection and privacy of the women she worked with.

I typed in Google: *How are Manitou and Manitoba related?* Manitou is situated in the Canadian province of Manitoba. It is an unincorporated urban community that previously held town status before January 1, 2015. It is surrounded by Mennonite communities and its one and perhaps only historical site is St. Andrews Church, built in 1901. I closed the Internet page and continued reading my notes.

"Some Indians were friends with the French. Some were friends with the Spanish, others with the English. During the big war, the Indians fought with each other because they were the only ones there. When the fighting was over, and the Indians wanted to return, the Americans would not allow them to do so."

"Why?" I asked.

"Because they had an alliance with King George at that point. So the natives had to stay in Canada." He paused before adding, "People in the clan system are still here. They haven't gone anywhere. It's the Sleeping Bear. It's sleeping because you're not using it. There are powerful things there, but no one uses them."

A group of women in saris walked in. They wore colors ranging from gold, green, red, and blue. They had children with them. Their men were already seated at separate tables. The place was loud, louder than usual. It was more challenging to focus on my notes, even after a second shot of coffee.

"They can say little bears were frolicking around there, whatever," said the Oneida Man. "But the Sleeping Bear is always here. It never left. It's still waiting for good things. And these people that make war don't want to wake up the Sleeping Bear because then the truth will come out."

"What do you mean?"

"The power of the air—radio, TV, advertising—has made people do whatever their next-door neighbor does. Living in this society and staying close to the earth is hard." He coughed for a while, and when he could speak again, he said, "The clan system holds you back, and most native elders know that. You can't tell younger people that. Some people are seventy, but they're as childish as a twelve-year-old. Yet they think they're the head of the clan. If you tell them they're not the head of the clan, they'll come on you like bricks."

"So, how do you handle that?"

"It's not your job to tell them they're not the head of the clan. It's their Creator's job to put it in their mind. If He doesn't put it in their mind, they don't have it anyway. I can tell you all sorts of things, Weam, but unless the Creator shows you, it's not real in your life. You can't help people that don't want the Creator's help. Really, you can't."

My eyes took a break and looked up. Two hijabi women sat across from me. One of them wore a burqa, a veil for the face that only left the eyes visible. She held the coffee cup in her right hand, pulled the niqab away from her mouth with her left hand to create a gap between her lips and the fabric, and took a sip. She repeated this a few times. The doorbell chimed, bringing my attention back to my work.

"There are people who are very, very old who are very, very young spiritually," said the Oneida Man. "And the rich ones are the most dangerous because they think they can buy everything, and they can. It's an uncomfortable place, but at the same time, you have to be cordial and understand."

He coughed a severe cough, and it took a while to clear his throat.

"You have to take it slow," he said. "It's fun to talk to someone who understands what you're saying without saying half a sentence. Have you ever run into someone like that?"

"Yes."

"That's what I'm saying. Some people don't understand what you're saying and are older age-wise but much younger spiritually. There are people in your community, in your church, that are running your community, like children. And natives are not any different than other people on the planet Earth. But the people who came here and started doing what they were doing, man, they were funny people. They had an agenda, and it was for the riches. It was for the commodities in the ground, and they'd do anything for it."

"Are they still doing that?" I asked.

"Yes. People don't want to go to Mars to enjoy the planet but to take what they can get, plunder the entire place, and get out of there. They don't even know what they're after but want to find out what's up there. They're spending millions and millions and going around with cruisers and all sorts of crap. It's just one big mine project to them, and they're exactly like the people who came here. They have no intention of living a clean life. They have no intention to live a life of good intentions. They intend to get as much as they can and die doing it."

A Chaldean man with a shaved head walked into the

coffee shop. He was dressed in black and wore a large cross. He looked familiar, but I didn't think too much of it, returning to my notes.

"Same with the fishermen in Alaska," the Oneida Man continued. "They're not out there for a good life. They're not happy until they get all the fish, all the fish and make lots of money. Same with the forests and hunting. Then they put it on TV, think they're funny, and make a big show about it. Then they have Tyson chicken advertising while you watch these guys plunder the North continent, and they think they're all fine."

A woman in a green burka walked in with her young children; the little girl wore a black burka, and the boy had on a T-shirt and shorts. A couple followed, walking side by side, laughing and chatting.

"They have to justify them coming here as pioneers by rewriting history," said the Oneida Man. "They say that Natives came from Mongolia when Natives were here when Mongolians moved here. That's why there's the DNA. I have European DNA, but it doesn't mean I came from Europe. I've never been to Europe. I don't plan to go there. It's because Europeans who came here enjoyed the company of others and they had children. When white people started the colonies, there were thousands of Chinese, and Mongolians, and Russians living here, also blacks and Europeans.

"They came here and said they own everything. If I go to live in Africa, I'm not going to live like an American. I'll live like an African. Same in Russia, same in China. When white people came, they brought their religion and said, 'I don't have to live like native people.' It wasn't the people who did that, it was the kings and queens. They took men out of prison and brought them here to do their job with the thirteen colonies. All the stories you hear about the thirteen colonies are like man going to the moon. It's not exactly how it was written."

Our histories shared many similarities. Our groups were forcibly displaced from their traditional lands and homes. Native Americans were forced to relocate to reservations or other areas designated by the US government, while Iraqi Christians suffered persecution and forced displacement from their ancestral lands. Both groups endured genocides by their invaders. These genocides involved efforts to destroy the culture and way of life of the targeted group. For Native Americans, this included forced assimilation into European-American culture through policies like the Indian boarding school system. For Chaldeans, Assyrians, and Syriacs, this included the destruction of churches, monasteries, and other cultural institutions, as well as the banning of the Aramaic language.

The differences between our groups are the length of time each experienced genocidal acts and the length of denials and cover-ups thereafter. Native Americans endured genocide over a period of several centuries. Christian Iraqis endured genocides and other forms of violence and for some 1,500 years. The US government has taken several steps to try to repay Native Americans for the harm done to them. The Iraqi government has done little, if anything, and Christians' survival in that land continues to diminish every day. On July 15, 2023, Patriarch Louis Sako announced in an open letter the decision to withdraw from the patriarchal headquarters located in the

Iraqi capital, Baghdad, and settle in one of the monasteries of the Kurdistan region. The last time a Chaldean leadership fled Baghdad was in 1259 A.D. due to the Mongols taking control of the city. One day, I'm afraid, we'll be reduced to three people, the number of Jews said to be left in Iraq.

"That's why they want to get rid of your language because there's so much history in your language. 'Oh, we can't understand what happened to all the Aztec people, why they just left,'" he imitated. "Well, you came to kill us, for a bowl. It was easier to leave than to deal with it. Plus, there was nothing there anyway."

I laughed, half-heartedly.

"Seriously, it was a freakish jungle," he said. "Then you have a picture in the Smithsonian by Catlin of an old man, saying how wise the guy is and the guy is not even there. He's already out there and might just come back for an hour or so to see the kids. The guy is out there, he doesn't care. He's almost gone."

I could not suppress blown-out laughter. Though I did not know Catlin and had not seen his artwork, I appreciated the Oneida Man's willingness to speak his mind and say what he truly believes. I appreciated that he looked within for knowledge and questioned things rather than take them at face value. It took a lot of discipline and will to do that.

Once the laughter dissolved, I asked, "Why is it difficult for people to live a good and spiritual life?"

"When you try to live a good and spiritual life, then the negative side works twice as hard to make sure that you don't. So you have to walk that fine line in between. When you step on people's toes, they try to dis your name, dis you as a person, and you have to deal with all that crap instead of caring for your mom and the kids."

He was referring to my lifestyle, as a mother of two children and the caregiver of my mother who lived with us, was in a wheelchair, and had dementia.

"You don't have to judge that," he said, "but you have to be aware of your environment. It's hard to do that sometimes. You think you can help, but you're not helping by suggesting solutions because unless the Creator puts it in their mind, they don't want to hear it."

"How do I talk to people without stepping on their toes?"

"I know not to elaborate on anything greater than what they can think about in their mind," he said. "When you pass away, you don't pass away with the community. You pass away by yourself and with the Creator. The community, the Earth, and everything around you are to benefit you and the Creator, but there comes a time when it's just you and the Creator."

CHAPTER 7

The Worlds of Corn and Honey

It was the month of May. We arrived at my cousin's unfinished house with a huge backyard. It was initially a tiny ranch built in 1947 during World War II. The woman who lived in it died, and her nephew sold it after he had cleared most of it of the furniture and her items. Some items, such as a vintage refrigerator, luggage, a yearbook, photographs, and laced curtains, remained. My cousin and her husband bought it to demolish it and build a much bigger house. They cut down the trees in the backyard. They began building a two-story extension, starting with a garage on the first floor and three bedrooms on the second floor. They turned the garage into a kitchen until the city approved the house design, and further construction continued. They turned the backyard into a little farm.

"We got new chickens. They're still babies," my cousin, Amy, said as she led me to the chicken coop, which housed ten brown and black chicks. "We put a fence on the top so the birds and raccoons can't get to them this time."

The last chickens they kept had more unique colors like white, red, and polka dot feathers. They were attacked and killed. Amy pointed to a wood slab against the fence. "We buried Skyler there," she said, referring to their dog, who died at five. Two motorcycles were parked near the corner, and beside them, stacks of material for a future shed.

Amy showed me the marks of two tree stumps recently removed. Then we walked to the built-in brick firepit. Her husband, Eddie, threw wood into it and started a fire. Several family members sat around the fire and told stories. The sun began to set.

Though it still required a lot of labor, perhaps years' worth of laboring, Eddie was incredibly proud of his home because it reminded him of his life in Iraq, or as we say, "back home." Crows cawed as he expressed his love for the simple life and living in nature. He felt he had the best of both worlds. He lived in the city, but the house felt like a farm with seclusion and acres of land. Everyone shared memories of the fruit trees that flourished in Iraq, from pomegranates to figs, apples, oranges, tangerines, plums, etc. My husband talked about how our ancestors farmed in Telkeppe, the village with primarily Chaldeans in northern Iraq. They grew whole grains and barley every other year to give the land a break. They grew watermelons, cantaloups, and cucumbers during the break year.

"I went to Telkeppe only once," said my older sister, Niran. "Grandma Amoona lived in a one-room house and had her appliances and whatever she needed there. It was on the second floor. On the first floor was the barn where the cattle stayed, like the cow and donkey."

Most homes in Telkeppe had an outhouse and tanoor, a clay oven, either on the rooftop or fifty to a hundred feet near the house. Many people shared an outhouse and tanoor. Few had refrigerators, and their way of cooling food and water was to place it in clay pots. When making yogurt, they buried the clay pot underground; when they retrieved it, it was as cold as ice cream.

The smoke from the fire drifted in our direction, and my husband jokingly cussed Eddie out. Eddie waived the smoke with cardboard. The atmosphere transported me to the day I visited a rhubarb farm where the Oneida Man lived. This was exactly twenty years ago, in May of 2003. He had told me that his family was nearly millionaires. His brother had invested in something that would double the speed of technology and make it cheaper. From the Internet to TV to telephone service, everything. His brother had been working on this for seven years, and now he would finally enjoy its fruits.

"Me and my family, including you, because you see, you helped me a great deal," he said at the video store.

"I did?"

"Yes. I came to you when I was dying, and you agreed to rescue me."

I once again didn't recall doing any deeds like these. "How did I do that?"

"By becoming a friend, an authentic platonic friend."

He sensed my questioning expression and said there was proof. "I can show you," he said, inviting me to his house for fresh tomatoes and rhubarb cake.

I went. He lived on a farm with a stove that burned wood for heat and a washhouse to wash beets, carrots, and other crops. The farm had an orange barn with a gray roof and a hammock attached. A white bunny with black fur around the eyes sat near a robin's nest. "It fell, so the parents left it," said the Oneida Man about the nest. We walked over scattered dry maple leaves. He pointed to the sunflower stalks and explained how they could reach nine, ten feet. "When they're ready, I remove the sunflowers and roast them."

Inside the barn was an old blue vehicle, an antique, a 1970 Dodge Dart. He fixed cars and sold them for a living. He showed me a book about the Dodge Dart and told me that this model was made from 1963 to 1976. He had a vehicle from an airport. It'd caught on fire. Airplanes stored food in that vehicle, then it went up high and into the aircraft. He was fixing it and selling it for $15,000 to builders.

Then we went into the house to eat spaghetti with homemade sauce. His daughter was there, about my age, and she and her young daughter joined us for dinner. He talked about various things. He gave me instructions for making a rattle. "Take out the squash pulp and rinse the inside with salt and water. Leave it out to dry for a few days, stuff it with black beans, stick a wooden handle, and you have a rattle."

His daughter and granddaughter didn't stick around for the rhubarb cake he served for dessert. The cake had crimson-red pieces of rhubarb and black raisins on top. I had no idea what rhubarb was. He explained what it looked like and brought in a stalk from the fields. It resembled celery with variations of pink, green, and red. It tasted bitter and weird in my mouth. He suggested I add salt, then said the middle part was best, pealed the stalk with a knife, and handed it to me. The cake was delicious. I had a slice and a half with my coffee.

There was a canteen on his kitchen wall made of

aluminum. "Before aluminum was introduced to the public around the 1930s," he said, "army men used canteens to store water. They had to return it once they completed their duties. World War I, that's how old it is." He also had an old doorknob, bedpost, and sand shovel—all metal. And three wooden signs, one with a picture of two strawberries, one that said the finest California grapes, and the third was of some company name. There were tiny and inedible boxes of produce and lots of decorative corn. "People could use them as beads to make bracelets and things," he said.

In the family room, in the corner, was a desk with a computer and a wooden oven where he destroyed his junk paper. "It's the gas tank of a truck, upside down," he said. "I slanted it on the ground, and the smoke goes outside the house. In winter, it makes the room very nice and warm. After a shower, I'll sit next to it."

"Who cooks?" I asked.

"Restaurants," he said and added that he knew how to cook. They got pizza on five-dollar days.

There was a round picture behind his desk. He bought it from a friend because the friend needed money. But he didn't like the cow head. It was an ugly picture. The picture was a man's back, riding a horse. Feathers dangled from the rim.

He showed me the pool room and told me how we first met. He recited the story of his encounter with the cops, his stay in the hospital, his repeated deaths, and finally, his visit to Video Castle. Before I left his home, he handed me boxes of accounts of his stay at the hospital. I showed these files to the doctor I worked for at that time. The doctor confirmed this patient had died. His heart stopped.

That evening suddenly felt like yesterday as I closed my memory and lay on the backyard rocking bench. The sun beamed over me, and a bird flew south. By now, my cousin and her husband were inside the garage preparing dinner. My husband left to have dinner at his mother's house. My sister put on her sunglasses and leaned back in her chair. She looked like a movie star in her long yellow dress.

What did the Oneida Man's hospital report mean? Could what he had said be true? He had died, and I helped bring him back to life? An odd story, indeed, I thought as I fell asleep and dreamt of my ancestors. Had they imagined, in a million years, that their grandchildren, including the girls, would one day live in two-story homes, each person having their bedroom, their car parked in the driveway, and a phone that weighed less than half a pound to carry around? They would have advanced appliances, including a machine that instantly made individual coffee cups? To them, this would have been the Twilight Zone.

"Weam, come eat dinner," I heard my cousin call. I opened my eyes and stared at the sky. I decided to call the Oneida Man once I arrived home.

At home, I brought cabbage, garlic, cauliflower, turnips, and beets to the kitchen counter to make pickled vegetables. I set the iPhone on speaker and called the Oneida Man. The ringing continued for a long time, and then there was a clicking sound.

"Well, how are you?" he asked, as usual skipping the "Hell O."

"I'm good," I said.

"I haven't heard from you for a while."

"I tend to take off, not sure where I go."

"Like Sabrina, the teenage witch?" he joked.

"I guess. I'm busy, but I don't run around doing things. It's mostly at my home and with my family."

"You have everything you need."

"I've been a hermit," I said.

"No, don't say that about yourself. A hermit is like an older person who's upset at everybody. He wants to stay inside because everyone is so ignorant and, 'Oh, I'm way above you, so why would I come out to talk to you?' It's self-professed studies. The Hermitage Club."

"Never heard of the Hermitage Club."

"You haven't?" he asked, acting surprised. "It's reserved for people who think they're greater than you are, the aristocrats. They keep to their heritage and can't socialize with normal people. That's the way I look at it. I might be wrong."

"I'm not aware of them," I said, peeling garlic.

"They're not as prevalent as they used to be. They were just a club that normal people couldn't go to."

"I thought that a hermit wanted to stay at home."

"No, that's a troll." He laughed. "Well, I'm a hermit."

"You're a hermit for sure."

"Why would I come out to talk to that person?"

"I was just thinking of the 1970 Dodge Dart you had at the rhubarb farm."

"Oh yeah, I fixed a lot of cars. That one made lots of money. It was blue and in good shape. Instead of writing books, I fix cars and sell them."

"If you fixed a lot of cars, how do you remember that one?"

"I have a photographic memory. There's a lot of noise in the background."

"It's the TV. I'm watching Say Yes to the Dress."

"I don't know that show. I've been watching Dr. Henry Gates Jr. on PBS. It's a six-hour program on Africa's history and pretty truthful. It's a way to help blacks assert their identity and self-worth, which they need to do. Black people kill each other like crazy. Dr. Gates didn't mention the corn we gave Africa when they had nothing. When I say we, I mean the North Americans, not me. I wasn't there at the time."

I poured turmeric and salt over the chopped cabbage, cauliflowers, and garlic and mixed them with a spoon. Then I stuffed the vegetables in jars and added equal water, vinegar, and apple juice in each jar.

"This goes back to Cleopatra's Dark Dance which I told you about, where it became cloudy and dark, with no sun and nothing to eat. America fed the world with corn. We just came through the time of corn and into the time of honey."

I wiped the mess caused by the cabbage and cauliflowers and prepared the jars of pickled turnips and beets.

"Did you know that?" he asked as I carried the jars to the basement in a large tub. I had to make two rounds. They would remain there for two to three days before being brought back upstairs and placed in the refrigerator.

"No, what's the time of corn and honey?" I asked.

"You don't know about that? I thought I told you about it."

Thus began a talk about corn and honey. I washed my hands, finally sat down, and began to take notes. He said that people only eat some of the corn that's growing. There are miles and miles and miles of corn, and most of it is not edible. It's hard and made into a commodity. The United States grows over 90 million acres of corn yearly, and 90 percent is unfit for human consumption. It's called field corn or cow corn and is fed to cattle, but mainly it's used to make plastic. Corn kernel grains can be turned into a plastic fork. Unlike plastic made from oil, corn plastic is biodegradable, carbon neutral, renewable, and even edible, but it is still surrounded by controversy. Since the mid-1990s, the world has headed toward honey. Instead of people working with their hands, they work with their minds. It's moving to a methodical method of spirituality.

"You know why it happened?" he asked.

"No."

"Because I said so," he said in a serious tone, then laughed hard. "Isn't that funny?"

"So none of this is true?"

"It is true. But it's because of me and others like myself."

"How long will the world be in the stage of honey?"

"Until people smarten up," he said. "It was really bad before, a dark-industry age. It killed the earth. This new age will be kinder to the earth, and more methodical thinking instead of just blasting and killing whatever is in front of you to eat everything up. Industry is selfish. It's not good to destroy things to make them good for yourself. 'What can I stack up in my garage for me?'" he imitated what a greedy person might think. "But things are changing."

He said there had been a continuous war for 2000 years, with one king here and there taking over several countries, over land, silk, and gold. "Corn is good, but what people do with it can be poor," he said.

Native Americans have cultivated beans, corn, and squash for thousands of years in Eastern North America. European settlers found this food new when some 400 years ago, natives began sharing it with them. Sources claim that corn was unknown in Mesopotamia, yet the Chaldean priest Berosus stated in his first book that corn and many edible things grew wild near the Tigris and Euphrates rivers, where the land was fertile. People of different races lived a sensual life. Berosus lived during the time of Alexandre the Great, and he wrote three books in Greek on the history and culture of Babylon, dedicated to the Greek King Antiochus (around 290 BC). Maria Theresa Asmar also wrote in great detail about Chaldeans growing corn in abundance. Later, I learned that the term "corn" in the Bible does not refer to Indian corn. It's likely that Berosus and Asmar were referring to the British word "corn" which implies wheat, rye, oats, and barley—grains that are common in that land.

"Let's see what they do with honey," said the Oneida Man. "Maybe they'll do bad with it, but at least they'll think about it first—not one guy assaulting another because of leaves blowing into his lawn. That's not methodical. That's like drug-related crazy. Children wouldn't even do that."

In the United States, Michigan was the center of honeybee

queen raising. More clover honey was produced in the Thumb than anywhere else and much of the early honeybee research was done at Michigan State University. Today the Michigan Beekeepers' Association is the oldest continuous bee association in the country. Honey has been noted in Babylonian and Sumerian writings as far back as 2100 B.C.E. when they began to farm. They also harnessed the power of the bees to produce honey for themselves. Honey was commonly used in pharmaceuticals to make medicine that also included herbs and botanicals.

"Soybean is like corn," he said. "It's a commodity. The ingredients of practically every product say soy or soy oil. Look at the cans on your shelves. I guess you use it as viscosity, like a base, a thickening. It thickens soup or any food—even pancakes. You can use it for plastic or cattle corn. Not all corn can be used for plastic. Soy is used more with vegetables and cooking.

"We designed corn to be eaten and we gave it to the whole world. I say we, meaning Native Americans, North Americans." He paused, then said, "Dr. Gates hasn't mentioned that in the PBS program. I could probably help him, but he hasn't asked. We gave corn to Africa when they had nothing to eat after the dark dance. There was nothing to eat. Corn came from here originally. North America fed the world with corn. We will feed the world with methodological thought and hopefully spiritually instead of killing each other over a set of car keys."

I listened, intrigued.

"Or am I wrong?" he asked.

"What?"

"That's what older people said when looking into my eye," he said, then imitating, added, 'How the hell would I know? You're the one saying it.' And Dr. Gates… I don't know where he got his doctor from. Many people say they're doctors. Maybe he's a rapper, a bubble gum wrapper." He laughed. "The Europeans were interested in gold, silk, fine clothes, and of course, sugar, commodities like that. That's why they enslaved people to work for nothing. Some slaves had a good life, I heard from elders. They had a house and didn't mind their life as opposed to figuring things out for themselves. Of course, I wasn't there, and I wasn't in the fields talking to them. I heard from elders."

"How long is it going to take for this change to happen?" I asked.

"I'm not the guy to ask that. I just know it's time to change. People know it's time to change."

He repeated that things are changing but added, "It doesn't sound like that with the guy that was in office. There must be something behind him. You can't act like that and be in the office." He was quiet momentarily and said, "Well, I guess you can."

I chuckled.

"That goes along with what I've been saying. They have a guy on a stick saying we're going to fight about this forever, fighting about who put him there. I don't know what they're fighting about. You have to be methodical and act. Are you writing this?" he asked.

"Of course."

He laughed so hard it caused a prolonged deep cough

that sounded like choking. He said between his coughing, "I can see you sitting there with your notebook."

"Yes, that's me."

"Does it fit into your story?"

"Of course."

"What do you call me in your books? The Red Native or Red Something…"

"The Red Indian," I said and told him that through my writers' groups, I learned that the Red Indian is a slur word offensive to Native Americans. "What are your thoughts on it?"

"Who gives a shit about that? If that's all I would have to worry about, I'd be happy. Some white people don't like to be called white. They want to be called Caucasian."

"Why is there such a negative feeling about the Red Indian?" I asked.

"All this goes back to racism, and because we're not the Indians the Europeans were referring to. Everything I told you—you must be methodical to see all this. It's not going to collide with your life if you're busy. You have to sit and watch; sometimes, understanding takes a long time. Your mother was methodical. Her method was to teach you, but you took a long time to see it.

"The world can heal itself. It can. It does. But people don't let it. They try to interfere. The people who take care of the fish want to heal the fish. Quit dumping shit in the water, and they'll heal themselves."

The phone ready to die, my husband having come to bed, the children—well, they were supposed to be in bed—the conversation with the Red Indian ended. I considered my notes, one dated Monday, October 18, 1999: I was watching the Discovery Channel last night and saw an Indian tribe where everyone walks naked and lives outdoors, surrounded by nature. One family the program focused on was made of a wife and her four husbands. There was such intimacy between the children, adults, and elders, so much playfulness and purity. When I turn to another channel, I see absurd gestures and many mind games. Noises everywhere, yelling, commanding, begging, blaming, advertising. I return to the tribe and am at peace again. Intimacy—between parents and children, husbands and wives, neighbors even.

I look at my current notes. My writer's group felt I need to bring myself into the story to ground it, since he's so out there. Some of their feedback included: after listening to you read, I feel more worldly. When you read, I'm not only entertained, but I always learn something. The facts filter through without us feeling bored by them. The way you bring us into the backstory is wonderful. They encouraged me to use the "Red Indian" title describing my friend if that felt right; after all, it was part of my Middle Eastern culture. Stay true to who you are.

Based on conversations with my Native American friend and my own research, I learned that many native tribes categorize the human race by the following colors: black, red, yellow, and white. Natives, also known as Indians, grouped themselves as red. So, wouldn't that make the term "Red Indians" a distinction rather than a slur? I have not received a clear answer to this question but rather countless opinions. It seemed that trying to be mindful of everyone's perspectives and experiences was impossible. It could cost one their voice. At the end, I gave the Red Indian the title of his tribe so as not to take focus away from the story, which is what political correctness does.

CHAPTER 8

Twenty-Year-Old Journal Entry

When I reached Haraz Coffee House in the late afternoon, the sun was still beaming through the windows. The strong aroma of roasted coffee beans greeted me, along with traces of cardamon, cinnamon, ginger, and even honey. I sat at the sunniest table in the establishment and began to unpack my briefcase of a laptop, paperclipped chapters, pens, pencils, and a thick yellow highlighter. For a moment, I observed the place, decorated with its Yemeni ambiance and the heat and energy familiar to the Middle East. It had a modern chic theme with a touch of history, including adorned walls. One wall had a mural of artifacts such as an oud, camel, palm date tree, mosque, antique Arabic tea kettle, and other items. Another wall had a detailed description of the history of Arabic coffee:

> The World's First Coffee. Yemen is the birthplace of coffee where the term Arabica originated, the place which introduced the first taste of coffee to the world. It was in Yemen that the coffee plant was cultivated and developed into the beans and beverages we know today. The process of cultivating coffee beans has remained the same in Yemen or over 500 years. Small

family farms plant on terraced field carved into landscape. Plants are grown with no chemicals, beans are sundried. Yemeni coffee has a distinct flavor and aroma, caring notes of chocolate, cinnamon, cardamom –

Did they mean carrying instead of caring? I wondered and quickly shook this question away to focus on the task at hand; the conversation I had nearly twenty years ago with the Oneida Man, written in a journal entry dated August 1, 2003. The Oneida Man and I were having a conversation at the video store, with me sitting on my favorite chair facing the window. He stood behind the counter. Based on the journal, asking him something had taken me a long time. He encouraged me to do so and I explained, "It's not a question, it's a request."

"I'm honored—that you ask," he said.

"When I'm looking for a publisher for *A Mirror of Two Brothers*, will you pray for it?"

"I already have," he said naturally. "That's what I've been doing. If you do well, I'll do well because we're on the right path."

His words reminded me of Carlos Castaneda. In his book, *The Teachings of Don Juan: A Yaqui Way of Knowledge*, his shaman teacher Don Juan asked him the following question: "Does this path have a heart? If it does, the path is good; if it doesn't, it is of no use. Both paths lead nowhere, but one has a heart, the other doesn't. One makes for a joyful journey; as long as you follow it, you are one with it. The other will make you curse your life. One makes you strong; the other weakens you."

"I want to help you because you've helped me, and I haven't made you realize how much," said the Oneida Man. "I had a hard time telling you I pray for you. I talk to very few people. I mean few. You know what few means?"

"Two?"

"I talk to the Creator, and I talk to you."

"You said you hadn't tried to call me for a while. Did you notice that I wasn't here when you didn't call me?"

"Absolutely. But I had to take care of things, get things straight. That was a very, very, very, very, long winter for me. Very long. It was like two or three winters." We were silent. "Your request for that didn't need to be requested," he said, referring to the prayer. "It's already done. I thought you knew that. I'm not going to tell you what I do. I'm going to show you."

I said nothing.

"Your request is late," he said. "I pray for you every day. That you do well. I like to help you because we're on the same path. The reward is like how Montana feels. Do you know how Montana feels?"

"No."

"Yes, you do. He likes to be with you."

Montana, my nephew, was born the year prior. His family and I lived under one roof. I watched him come into this world from his mother's womb, named him, and will never forget that day.

"And that's enough?" I asked.

"Yes, it's like a child. When they're around you, they learn from you. When I'm around you, I take four steps forward." He said he liked to talk to me, but not over the phone. "The phone takes away spirituality. It takes away countenance…"

He paused, probably seeing from my expression that I did not know the meaning of countenance. "Look it up in the dictionary," he said, his eyes indicating the stack of books I had on the windowsill: a thesaurus that fits into my palm; a larger thesaurus that was first published in 1852, revised in 1937 and gifted from a Frank to a Janet in the Christmas of 1938 (I bought it used); a dictionary, fairly new in comparison, published in 1990.

I grabbed the dictionary, looked up countenance, and read the definition. When I finished, he said, "Your body language and countenance of yourself say what you're really saying—the truth. You hear what I say but you don't really see the spirit of it."

That journal entry ended. The sight of the black-dressed server walking around the café, looking lost, made me pause. *Could that be my drink?* I'd placed my table number near the windowsill, hidden behind my laptop and stacks of books and papers. He probably could not see it. I waived my hand and he, relieved, quickly brought over the specialty coffee with cardamom, cream, and sugar. One sip and the energetic effect caused me to be in a euphoric state. I observed my surroundings, inhabited by people speaking diverse languages from Arabic to Indian to, yes, English: a group of young Indian men and women gathered around one table; elegantly dressed Asian women sat with their children at another table; two black women sat on the couch, their dreadlocks reaching past their waists. They looked like mermaids. A baby girl crawled on the floor, accompanied by a girl toddler. Muslim hijabi women sat alongside Muslim non-hijabi women.

Surrounded by the enticing aroma, I finally returned my attention to the next journal entry dated Saturday, August 16, 2003. It consisted of one sentence: I had a dream; an old man dressed in a turban, looking like a Bedouin, said to me in Arabic, "*Rouhi hajiya, Allah maaij.*" Go hijiya, God is with you.

This journal entry always startles me no matter how often I read it. In Arabic, *hajiya* has several meanings: an honorary title for Muslim women who have completed the Hajj to Mecca and a word to show respect when addressing an elderly person. My husband started calling me that after we had two children, he claims, although I'm not sure when he started or why. One day, I asked him, and he said, "It's a word of respect for elderly wise women and because you *are* a hajiya. You went to the Holy Land." I Googled whether Christians used the word hajj when describing a person who made a trip to the Holy Land, Jerusalem, and according to Dictionary.com, my husband is correct. Since the sixteenth century, in Balkan countries under former Ottoman rule, some Orthodox Christians adopted this word for their own pilgrimage to the Holy Land.

A text pinged from my iPhone; a message from my son requesting an order from McDonald's. I smiled, then stood to stretch. I walked to the display counter with shelves of distinctly embroidered tea and Turkish coffee kettles, water pitchers, trays, and a few books, one on Yemeni architecture and the other called *Eight Days in Yemen* by Peter Schlesinger. Turning around to walk back to my table, I saw a painting on the wall of an old man with a long white beard. He dressed in Yemeni attire with a turban and a jambiya, a type of dagger, on the belt on his hip side. Behind him was a historic cityscape of old

Sanaa, Yemen's capital and largest city. The painting on the wall of the old Yemeni man resembled the man in my dream who said to me, "Rouhi hajiya, Allah ma'aij."

His image, along with Fairuz's song, playing faintly, caused my thoughts to be suspended in the air.

I love you, Lebanon
My homeland, I love you…
I love you in your poverty
I love you in your wealth
And my heart is in your hands
May your heart not forget me.

Servers dressed in black rushed to and fro holding trays of tea or coffee kettles and unique cups. The sound of a baby crying throbbed from a nearby table. I returned to my table, convinced that the old man and my husband calling me hajiya is no coincidence. Neither is my conversations with my Native American friend.

CHAPTER 9

The Ten Commandments

Snow covered the city with a white blanket, the result of last night's snowstorm. Everything was white: the rooftops, cars, swing set, porch chairs, table, tree branches, and hanging plant pots. The intense sun and warm temperatures quickly melted the snow into water piles. I took Teddy and my brother's dog, Prince, for a walk that wet our feet. Once home, I changed my socks and shoes, packed my computer bag with my laptop, books, and bound book chapters, and headed to Haraz Coffee House.

The place was packed. I sat on the brown leather couch and placed my stuff on a rustic low round coffee table. The space was distinguished from the rest of the seats. It looked like a cozy living room. I began to read a journal entry without a date. It took place sometime after I had visited the rhubarb farm. The Oneida Man was talking about the church's people, who represented male dominance.

"There has been a lot of imbalances for thousands of years," he'd said. "It didn't happen yesterday: five hundred years with Greece, five hundred years in Rome, five hundred years in the United States and Russia. China is working inward on inequality. It's hard to break that cycle after three thousand years of history when you lived and wrote it down that way and put it in the archive as they did and contribute to it through films and news, and they say how bad it is but uphold it anyway. If you're a maternal person, everything you say and do is geared against that."

I imagined myself sitting in that chair at the video store, listening in silence.

"Jesus is not about that," he'd said. "But remember, Jesus didn't write. He spoke. Others wrote, and when he spoke, others wrote what they thought he said. When they went to school, the paternal got a hold of them. It's paternal spirituality that wrote the books. I know it's sad, and it is sad, and it sounds doomed, but not really...."

The black-dressed server brought over my coffee and set it on the table. I thanked her and then took a sip while staring at the words on the wall about the history of coffee in Yemen. I looked up Haraz on the Internet. An article published by the Guardian showed an image of an old farmer in the fields with a handful of freshly picked ripe, red coffee cherries. Behind him, a glimpse of a medieval village lay in the distance. The article described how farmers at Haraz, a collection of medieval villages in Yemen's highlands, dried and aged coffee cherries once harvested and separated the beans from the husks by hand.

Since the 1400s, Yemen has been exporting coffee, which originated in Ethiopia but was developed by Sufi monasteries in Yemen into the modern drink we know today. These monasteries shared their coffee with traders and pilgrims, and it eventually spread to Constantinople (now Istanbul), Baghdad, and London. With a current worth of £61.4bn, the coffee industry is now the second most valuable trading commodity in the world after oil.

A few people walked into the coffee house. They spoke Hindi, I assumed, and they sat across from me. Soon other members of their family followed, ranging in age from a newborn baby boy to elderly couples. Evidently, they needed the square-shaped space resembling a living room, so I packed up my belongings and moved to a corner table near the window. I reread the part where the Oneida Man talked about Jesus speaking and the paternal spirituality and how this is sad but not really.

"This has been going on for thousands of years and causes an imbalance in life and death," he'd said. "Nature is hated, but nature creates the biggest balance. They made war on God, and they hate native because that's what God left as reality. God doesn't tap you and tell you that's how things are. He speaks to you through nature, and that's why they kill nature. Some animals no longer exist." He mentioned the wooly mammoth, Irish elk, ground sloth, and quagga. The quagga was half zebra, half horse. "Anyway, I'm not trying to make you feel bad. That's just the reality of it."

I must have said something, I know not what, because he said, "You ask inquisitive, good questions, and I would tell you these weren't what they valued or solved. I tried to help you on how to edit your work so you wouldn't be so conforming to the public. Before, you had a lot of degrees from history and university meaning to things. You did not know modern apples were domesticated from wild Asian apples and European crabapples. Eve enticed Adam with something other than apples, that's for sure." He nodded to himself. "Just information. A lot of natives lived there. That's where Pontiac lived."

"Where?" I asked.

"Apple Island. It's in Orchard Lake, and that's where Chief Pontiac lived. But his name was Obwandiyag. They misspelled it and mispronounced his name and called him Pontiac. It's like saying Weem instead of We'am. They're so disconnected from nature that they don't know their gender. They don't even know what they are or how to act. No one can save me from myself but myself. Nor any woman, for that matter. Still, in knowing, we become responsible."

"In knowing what?"

"That Jesus was our savior, who came and saved everyone, even the cats and dogs."

"How do you explain Jesus multiplying the fish?"

"I've never multiplied a fish, so I don't know. It's an idea, though." He laughed. "I feel the multitude is to teach people. To talk to people all at once. To break bread meant to have dinner. What I'm saying, friend, is there's more to life than religion."

"If Christianity's ways don't appeal to you, what does?" I asked.

"Living off the earth instead of changing it, that's what. Maintaining things so they don't change drastically. That's a natural person's ideal."

"I read somewhere that in most civilizations, the following groups exist, king or ruler, court, government, noblemen, priest, churches, medicine man, military, army, warrior. Within priests, there are healers, scribes, and prophets. It's the prophets that cry out at social injustices. They look at the cause and effect. They make people look at their actions. If each citizen heard them out, was patient with the message delivered rather than critical or suspicious, the prophecy, their vision, would be apparent and fulfilled."

"All religions are broken into many fragments," he said. "None of them are one solid belief. The problem is if you're sovereign, you say you and not God, not the higher power, not the sovereign Creator—have complete control over your destiny. All religions point to God. If they even mention Him, it's good as long as they realize its meaning is greater than they are."

"What are your thoughts on the Ten Commandments?"

"If you're in agreement, why would you command? Why would God have to command? Why are there nots in commandments? Nots are negative. God is not negative. People are negative. God is positive."

"What do nots create?"

"A fight. If you tell someone not to do something, they say why? If you tell someone to do something, they'll say, to what means? Everything about the commandments takes away from you as a person, reduces you as a person—by telling you not to. If I tell you, don't do that, it's in your nature to do it. Those who wrote the Bible don't have why not to. They replace the positive with negative and make you live by it, knowing you couldn't do it.

"For example, one of the Christian things is that people don't have sex without getting married first. But that's hard to live by. Nobody lives by it. They tell you there is sex by telling you not to have it. It's like a double negative, which equals a positive. See, people were given commandments because they couldn't live under direction. I live under myself."

He said those commandments are good, but they were not given to everyone. "They were given to people who were not following the rules and not relying on God. No one has to command me not to kill someone. I don't want to hurt anyone, much less kill anyone. No one needs to command me. Native people don't live under commandments. They are in agreement with their Creator. My Creator does not have to command me. If I have to be commanded, then I'm a very poor fellow. Those people who He gave those commandments were very poor, and that's why He gave the commandments to them. They were not in agreement with the Creator anymore."

He explained that the Ten Commandments were suggestive selling to ninth graders. "You suggest a product to them, show it, talk about it, or use it yourself. That's what the Ten Commandments are doing. They're suggesting. Don't do this, and don't do that. It suggests that you need this. Advertising suggests that people need this in their life, and it works because you have a lot of stuff you don't need."

"What's the difference between a consensus vs. law?"

"The difference between consensus vs. law is that the first says, hey, let's go for coffee. The second says, if you don't go for coffee, I'll have someone come get you."

"Are you saying that Christianity hasn't served us well?"

"Apparently not because we have a big mess. Christianity is based on things, not you getting better. It teaches you how to make more money, pay the church and your taxes, get a good job, etc. In France, taxes are very high. In most European countries, actually."

"Where does it say that in the Bible?"

"All you have to do is watch. Tarot cards, used during the Renaissance, were stopped by the church because they didn't want independent thought. They wanted people to turn to priests and the church. The Bible used to be locked up with a key at the Vatican because priests feared the public would read and misinterpret it. Of course, they were the ones who did the misinterpretation. Maybe you can't name them since, in the Bible, God told the Hebrews to kill the Palestinians. God never told me that. 'Oh, oh, but He told me.' This other guy will tell you. I say to him, 'Well, when He tells me, I'll change.'"

He was silent momentarily. "I'm not saying Christianity is bad," he said. "Nothing is bad in and of itself. Poison ivy is good as long as you don't get into it. But my point is no man on earth can save me from myself."

He began talking about the Tower of Babel. He said it was a tribute for people to remember to keep the land fertile. The tower had several layers of different flowers, fruit, and vegetables. "I'm not saying it was a shrine," he said, "but it was a remembrance to keep different food groups—a balance—so you and the land could stay strong and healthy. It was a standard of living. Christians say that Babylonians were heathens, ungodly. They say the tower was their way to get to God without the Bible. People say anything about those they don't like."

I reflected on his statements.

"There's very little nature left," he said. "That's what the Creator left for us—His Nature or Her Nature. Who said the Creator is He or a She, for that matter? But to prosper on the earth, they need it to be a He and She. There are animals in nature that are neither male nor female but became female when they gave birth. It isn't that any side is good or bad. People are people. They're the same."

"Why is there so much negativity?"

"Because of the imbalance—even in women. If there were only female in every kingdom and every home, it would be the same way it is now—backward and imbalanced. You could even be buried underground without a headstone over you."

"Where were Natives buried?"

"In a mound, all together. Now there's a block stuck on your head. And a cement spine for the whole family—ten feet and twenty feet tall."

I concluded that day at Haraz with these words by the Oneida Man: "In Genesis, people trace their patriarch heritage. Jesus' dad was not from a kingly family. The mother was. She was royalty. They killed him because he was preaching as if he were royalty."

A little research led to the following: The Gospel of Matthew describes Joseph as a carpenter (Matthew 13:55) and the Gospel of Luke describes him as a "son of Heli" (Luke 3:23), who was likely a commoner. Yet the Gospel of Matthew also states that Joseph was a descendant of King David (Matthew 1:1-16), through David's son Solomon. David received his kingship through prophetic appointment by Samuel. No one was permitted to sit on David's throne unless they were a member of the house of David. When there was a conspiracy to overthrow the house of David, God warned that it would inevitably fail. A problem with Matthew's genealogy results from what's stated in Jeremiah 22:24-30:

"As I live," says the Lord, "though Coniah the son of Jehoiakim, king of Judah, were the signet on My right hand, yet I would pluck you off; and I will give you into the hand of those who seek your life, and into the hand of those whose face you fear—the hand of Nebuchadnezzar king of Babylon and the hand of the Chaldeans. So I will cast you out, and your mother who bore you, into another country where you were not born; and there you shall die. But to the land to which they desire to return, there they shall not return. Thus says the Lord: 'Write this man down as childless, a man who shall not prosper in his days; for none of his descendants shall prosper, sitting on the throne of David, and ruling anymore in Judah.'"

According to Jeremiah 22:24-30, no descendant of Jeconiah would be eligible for the throne of David. This posed a problem for messianic lineage, as the Messiah was required to be both from the line of David and not from the line of Jeconiah. However, Joseph's lineage in Matthew's genealogy traces back to Jeconiah, which would disqualify any of his descendants from sitting on David's throne. This raises the question of how Jesus could be the Messiah if he came from the line of David but was also linked to Jeconiah. The solution to this problem lies in the Virgin Birth. Jesus was not Joseph's biological son, so the curse of Jeconiah did not apply to him. However, Jesus was still Mary's biological son through the Virgin Birth.

I packed up my stuff and left for home.

The chapter on the Ten Commandments was placed on hold until another afternoon at Haraz Coffee House. May 13 marked the day my father passed away thirty-seven years ago. This time, the sun was nowhere in sight, the sky was cloudy, and the weather was warm. I sat at a table with a gold tray belonging to the previous diners. A kettle, coffee cups, and plates of leftover chocolate cheesecake and silverware were on the tray. I carried the tray to the front counter and returned to the table to begin my writing. I acknowledged the old man in the large size painting, who resembled the old man in my dreams. I recalled his words, "Rouhi hijiya, Allah ma'ij."

I looked up the history of Yemen and found that for thousands of years, the country had been the world's most lucrative trade route. It connected Africa, the Middle East, and at times the Mediterranean to the markets of East Asia. According to legend, the biblical Queen of Sheba, consort of King Solomon, was Yemeni. Islam arrived in 630 CE, and Yemen became part of the Muslim realm.

I called the Oneida Man. The phone rang.

"How are you?" he asked, skipping the Hell O.

We exchanged greetings, chit-chatted a bit, and I asked, "What happened to the house and farm you used to live in, the one I visited?"

"They're gone," he said. "The house, farm, road, driveway, barn, everything is gone. It was a hundred acres, and now it's a subdivision with three-story homes, a public school, and an emergency medical center. You can do a Google Earth to see."

I looked up Romeo Plank, the main road the farm was on. I came across Romeo, the village in the same county, Macomb. The indigenous Chippewa originally occupied this land, thought to have migrated to the area by the twelfth century. They were Algonquian-speaking people. The early European-American settlers called the area Indian Village. Silas Scott cleared the first land here in 1821, and over the years, its name was changed to Romeo at the suggestion of Mrs. Laura Taylor because it was "short, musical, classical, and uncommon."

Though not named Indian Village, schools are called Chippewa Valley. Their names continue somehow, as it should, as the world claims it wants for the indigenous people. The UN's "Declaration on the Rights of Indigenous Peoples" validates the rights of any group to maintain, observe, and protect its culture and traditions. Of course, not everyone upholds this human right. I once read an article that ISIS, among the countless atrocities it committed, ransacked and burned the Mosul Public Library and destroyed over 8,000 antique and rare books and manuscripts. This tactic is known as "cultural genocide," the Islamic State militants employed it to turn the region into a single, homogenous Muslim caliphate under its control.

"I love this place," the man sitting near my table said to

a server. He was tall, large, and had a smirk on his face. "It's quiet, friendly, and serves tasty chai. It gets me out of the house, away from the kids. Kids drive you crazy. Here, I can think. At home, my brain stops." He stood up and put on his jacket. "It could be worse. I've been married for twenty years. Makes things easier. Some people had three, four marriages, like rabbits." He laughed. "Me, just once."

He walked out of the establishment, and my attention trailed off to the Arabic song by the Lebanese singer Elissa. Then to the people coming in and out of the coffee shop, a hijabi woman in a long dress holding a newborn. She waited for her husband to remove the stroller from the trunk and set the car seat over it. Then he placed the baby bag in the carry cart. I relished the aromas of cardamom, nutmeg, cinnamon, coffee, and pasties that filled the atmosphere. A group of people walked in, followed by more people ranging from babies in strollers to elderly with walkers. A professional photographer shot pictures. One child stopped at the door and refused to go inside. "I think he's scared," the father said.

They accumulated to at least four dozen individuals and took up half the coffee shop. Some wore white shirts that said, "Christina Hines" (in red fonts) and "for Macomb County Prosecutor" (in blue fonts). Four men placed a sign on the wall, over the history of Yemen writing, with those exact words. The sound inside Haraz grew louder than I'd ever heard before. A local representative, Lori Stone, spoke into the microphone. She introduced Christina and said a few words about having passion, stamina, and vision. People clapped. "This is the toughest race of her life, but she is in the right place, surrounded by people who love her."

The rain started falling. I had no further thoughts but only a sense of wellness and love for where the Creator had placed me.

CHAPTER 10

Jesus Was Here

The winter wind swept against my face, causing my hoodie to fall back. I again placed the hoodie over my head before I looked both ways and crossed the street. Teddy followed swiftly and happily, loving the cold like a child loves ice cream on a hot summer day. Although I come from a faraway land known for its hot temperatures, deserts, and sandstorms, I did not mind the cold. I arrived at this mysterious land exactly forty-two years ago. I've become accustomed to it and have grown to love the things I once thought strange and unpleasant such as the taste of pizza, wearing pants and gym shoes, and keeping dogs as pets.

I removed the glove from my right hand and called the Oneida Man. He answered and told me about a recent visit to the doctor. He said all was well and credited the time he got a good tune-up at the hospital twenty-six years ago. He referred to when he died four times and was resuscitated four times. How would I take notes of our conversation? The iPhone did not recognize human touch with gloves on. Despite the cold, I kept the glove off to type. "I'm now sixty-six years old and much older than you, old enough to be your father or brother," he said, reflecting on his age and health. "With the thought to take care of you."

I muted my phone so the sound of the wind would not disturb him.

"The tailor had the same sense to look out for you, and the way I know that is when I visited, he would watch me with good intentions." He laughed. "He was on the same ball."

His words took me down memory lane to the days I managed the video store. The tailor's shop was next to the video store. He would often stop in to say "Hi," say a few jokes, comment on how easy my job was compared to his, then leave after making complaints about life in general. His wife used to help him out and bring the children to the shop. His daughter had cancer and passed away in her twenties.

When my thoughts returned to the call, the Oneida Man was talking about numbers. "I remember back in the day, I knew fifty people's numbers, and now I can't even remember my own number," he said. "Of course, I can't even remember my own number. Of course, I don't call my number. I would remember numbers and equate them to their personalities."

"Where are you living now?" I asked, my lips barely able to move.

"I'm living on my sister's farm, an hour away. The other house was a loud place to live, with many motorcycles and trucks. It's quiet here. Lots of beer…"

"Beer?"

He repeated the word several times, and I finally said, "Oh, deer. I couldn't hear you. It's so cold and windy out here."

"There's wildlife here, kind of like retirement," he said.

"A lot of native people knew people were going to come and enjoy the place and live with us—prophecy. They thought it was good because the Creator said it, but the bad guys didn't do that. They killed and had dogs chase after them. The Europeans came looking for a better life, so a lot of people didn't fight. They wanted to enjoy stories, ideas, neighbors, and trade. Things didn't happen the way they were supposed to."

"Where is this?"

"It's biblical. God was not unique to the Middle East. People here were not ignorant of God. When Jesus came, he transformed religion from tradition to spirituality so you could pray every day and didn't need anyone to interpret for you—take a goat and slaughter it. The Bible is a guide. It would be better if they trusted God. That's why Jesus came. They preferred to preach and read but not go all the way, pay the full price of entry. Entry into the world of balance, whether they're working outside or in retreat."

"What keeps people from God?"

"I know nothing but that what separates most people is talk. How much of it is said and it's used makes a difference and whether a day comes where all the talk cannot do what an act has to."

My hands turned red and shriveled from the cold. The call ended before I arrived home. I called him later that night while sitting beside the fireplace.

"I hung up on you," said the Oneida Man. "I was trying to answer the phone, and it's dark. I was online and watching YouTube or whatever. I pressed the hangup button." He laughed. "It's cold outside. You went walking?"

"Yes, I go out with my dog. I make him wear a coat because he just had a haircut and loves jumping in the snow."

"My sister's daughter has a chihuahua but not a toy chihuahua. It has long legs and looks like a deer. It's the funniest dog you'll see. Runs on three legs and switches legs. It's a yappy mutt. It could be in a circus, it's so silly. If a leaf blows by, it starts barking at the leaf. If the wind blows, he barks. Anyway, you got your dog a coat because he got a haircut?"

"Well, he has pajamas, jacket, coat…."

He laughed.

"I watched the *Elder Brother's Warning*."

"I heard that they make a rope bridge and gather the bridge, roll it up, so you could not get there. You could if you had a helicopter, but you can't just walk there. That movie has been out for a long time. It's been so long, but I heard some of the people in the movie have died because of old age, and some were killed because of their beliefs and world views, I guess you'd say. There are people like that. They are nasty. But yeah, that group had a lot of older traditions of how they make things work for them. What you think is silly compared to what's real, like what a butterfly looks like and what it can do. Even if a good orator tells you what something is like, you see it, and your interpretation of it is crazy."

"I thought it was interesting how they refused to wear shoes," I said.

"The earth draws toxicities from your body through your feet. I know it's hard to believe because everyone wears shoes and walks on cement. Being barefoot is therapeutic. People find foot doctors for cleansing and muscle relaxation. I forget what the word may be. They can draw toxicities from your body and the sole of your feet. The earth does that when you walk barefoot."

"I know a lot of mothers who don't want their kids to walk on grass."

"People don't go to the beach until it's warm, and then the sand is so hot, their feet burn, so they wear sandals." He laughed. "Some people wait until they can't walk on the sand. Anyway, I'm just making a joke."

"Back home, we were encouraged to go out and play in the dirt."

"Like kids in the sandbox, it's good for you."

"Are you still living far away?"

"Yeah."

"Do you live alone?"

"I still live in my trailer." He explained it's parked in his sister's house, where several family members live. He told me his niece is getting married.

"Are you going?" I asked.

"Yeah, I paid for some of the…what do you call it?"

"The reception. Is it a totally American wedding, or do you include your traditions?"

"She's native, and he's native from Puerto Rico, and they have three children." He told me a little more about them, then I asked, "How did you get your last name?"

"From my dad, and he got it from his dad, and he got it from his dad. My dad's dad was from Scotland. We're native, but…"

"Wait a minute! You're partially European."

"Yeah, my grandfather was from Scotland. That's why I'm so fair."

I cracked up because I wouldn't necessarily describe his skin as fair.

"My mother's mother was from England, and my dad's dad was from Scotland. But my dad's mother was native. That's why I got mixed. My mother's dad is native. They were from North Carolina and moved to Oklahoma. My mom was half, and my dad was half, and that's what I'm saying. That's how you had to survive, man. It was pretty hard to survive with these people that came here. It was hard to live with them because they wanted to kill you, so you had to be like they were by marrying them, living with them… I'm not crying about it. I'm just saying."

"Will you wear a suit?"

"No, I'm going to be the bad uncle. I'm not a member of the wedding party or anything. I don't have to give her away or anything. I'm just the uncle." He later described his trailer. "It's a tiny house, and it's zero outside, seventy inside, and very warm. It's nice and warm and insolated. It has windows like a house. I enjoy it because it's small for me. It just fits me."

There was a moment of silence. I listened to the crackling fire.

"I always wondered," he said. "I used to build houses when I was younger before I did ironwork and welding, and the houses I built were ranch or two-levels. The houses now, why would you build a house that big? The neighborhoods have to conform to certain sizes of homes with the number of square feet. That's the same with my farm, the whole backyard, the field, and all that. I lived there for almost five years, which was good for me because it was cheap rent to live there. We were just renting. They had planned to do the subdivision from that time."

We brought up his mom.

"You met my mom at my niece's high school graduation party. It was at a house in East Pointe. We sat with her, and my sister, and other people came and went and talked to my mom and you. My sister had a heart attack and flatline; they brought her back. She's still with us, but she has to take care of herself a little better. Of course, my mom died in South Carolina. My sister bought her a house there, and my mom moved down there and ended up dying down there."

"What did she die of?"

"She died of a golf ball size cancer in her head," he said. "Her death certificate says due to cigarette smoking because they need that statistic, so they don't mention the real cause. My mother never smoked a day in her life. Tobacco is one of the most pure things on earth. It's what they put in the cigarettes, how they process and market the tobacco that's the problem. They bleach the paper, filters, and stuff that makes it go out when you're not smoking. Tobacco is the best part about it. But they have to demonize stuff because of cancer."

I recalled his mother's kind face and the delicious rhubarb cake she baked.

"Our family was pretty tight," he said. " We did a lot of things together. For the graduation, my niece wanted all her aunts, uncles, and everyone. Her friends from school came and visited the family."

"I remember one of your sisters coming to the video store a lot with her husband."

"Her daughter, her daughter's husband, and my brother live with her, and I have my little house outback. She's elderly and had a stroke, but she's not as bad as my brother. I mean, we're elders over here." Laughed. "I'll be sixty-seven this year."

"When I was young, I visited this family that was Bedouins, I believe. I remember a tent and a bonfire and me just looking at them, and they looking at me. We visited in silence…."

"Like a silent family."

I drank my hot cocoa during a moment of silence.

"I quit smoking a year and a half ago, and I didn't have much energy, so I went to the doctor, who said I have high blood pressure. When things were happening with my family, I said I better go and check myself. I didn't quit because of my sisters and brothers and all their ailments; I quit because I wanted to quit. I started smoking at sixteen when I left home because I wanted to be a big shot. I feel better because I quit smoking, but at the same time, it's change. It's just age, man. I used to help the elders, and now I need help."

I told him we'd catch up one day over coffee.

"Okay, but we'll have to catch up slowly," he said.

"Yeah, I've learned over the years I can work more efficiently if I slow down, although I still tend to want to go fast."

"My dad used to say, 'Your mind says, *go, go, go* and your body says *no, no, no.*' Now it's a reality for me. The kids used to be the kids, and now they have kids. My daughter in Canada has a granddaughter. When they got bigger, it was odd."

"Yeah, and mine started calling me names, like 'Karen.' I was like, 'Who's Karen?'"

"What do they call guys, Karen too? I think Karen, too, but I've been called a lot worse. My one grandson is thirty years old. I'm a great grandpa too. I told all of the kids, 'My dad never jumped in a car to visit the kids. I took my kids to see my dad.' I'm not trying to play role reversal or nothing. But anyway, life goes on. He didn't chase my kids or anything."

We were quiet.

"I miss my boy," he said. "Drugs got him. You remember him?"

"Yeah. He was a gentleman and always smiled."

"You need to hug your kids, tell them how much you care about them. Okay, Karen, I'll let you go."

I laughed. "Okay, Karen, will talk to you soon."

CHAPTER 11

The North American

My husband and I headed to Grand Rapids for our eighteenth anniversary. He wanted to take me there because of the museums downtown and the bridge overlooking the river. I agreed so long as I chose the hotel. I found Amway Grand Plaza Hotel, which overlooks the Grand River. Originally named Pantlind Hotel, it opened in 1913, the year of President Gerald R. Ford's birthday and the first year of the income tax. Their website said it had one of the world's largest twenty-four-karat gold-leaf ceilings and the most stunning chandeliers in the lobby.

"That's where I want to stay," I told my husband, booked a room with a river view, and we started packing. I placed in my tote bag my flowery 2023 planner and a green journal with Frida Kahlo drawn on it. Frida is wearing a pink scarf, pink flowers over her dark hair, and pink lipstick. She has on a white pearl necklace and white glove-shaped earrings. A blue and gold bird sits on her right shoulder. I included my Aramaic language book and a yellow folder with the words "The North American by Weam Namou." That was one of the many titles I had acquired for this book over the years.

I skimmed through the loose papers in the yellow folder

in the car. They consisted of paperclipped chapters and notes about my conversations with the Oneida Man. One conversation I had tried to turn into a poem the way I had with *Love, Justice, and Turtle Soup*. The attempt was unsuccessful. I called the poem *Pomme*, the French word for apple.

"Do you know why the French call it pomme?" the Oneida Man asked.

"Why?" I asked.

"Because they know the origins of an apple. It's made from a bush and a hawthorn tree. A hawthorn tree is pretty in spring, it blossoms nice, but it can't be eaten. All its parts are poison. So people got rid of the thorn and made crabapple. An apple is not that old. They depict it as though it was always here since biblical times. It wasn't always here. There's a theory that the tomato got Adam and Eve out of Eden. An apple is good. But they depict it as though Allah made it, and that's what's bad."

He normally used Creator or God, but this time he used the Arabic word that's associated with that land. Although, the biblical term was Aramaic, *Allaha*. A pomegranate came to mind, a word from the medieval Latin *pomum*, "apple" and *granatum*, "seeded." The old French word for the fruit is pomme-grenade. No one knows if the "forbidden fruit" in the biblical Garden of Eden was a pomegranate, a fig, a grape, or any fruit. Some claim it was palm dates, Iraq's national symbol, which are also a favorite aphrodisiac in that region. Dates are served along with yogurt, a sleep-inducer, to grooms on their wedding nights.

I closed the folder and blankly looked out the car window.

Long car or airplane rides gave me the sense of sitting in a rocking chair, surrendered to a state of stillness with eyes wide open to the world's movement.

We checked into the hotel, then my husband and I walked to the Grand Rapids Public Museum. We arrived at 4 pm and had one hour to look around, with a free carousel ride at 4:40 pm. "Who walks through a whole museum in one hour?" I asked.

"We can skip the carousal ride," my husband said, grinning.

"No." I had not been on a carousal since before the pandemic. I used to ride them with the kids at Greenfield Village and wanted to revisit the experience.

The museum consisted of three floors. The first floor showed what life was like in the late 1800s in Grand Rapids. A firetruck that operated on a steam engine, a train station with arrival and departure times written on chalkboards, a grocery, a printer, and other shops based on actual buildings. One exhibit showcased ancient Egyptian artifacts, including the mummy of a woman, Nakhte-Bastet-Iru. Another exhibit had above its entrance door a large photo of five generations of Anishinabek women and the words: We are the Native American people of West Michigan: We call ourselves the Anishinabek, the "First people," the Ottawa (Odawa), Potawatomi, and Chippewa (Ojibwa) Indians of Michigan.

"I'll need to come back tomorrow," I said, mesmerized.

We rode the carousel, dated 1928, and returned to our hotel in the rain. After we checked out of our hotel the following day, my husband and I headed to the museum. We had coffee and shared a sizeable Macedonian cookie at the museum café. Then began our tour, or at least mine. He sat on blue sofas waiting for me as I traveled from object to object, engrossed in the Native American history and stories that resembled my people's.

A rack of forty-eight baskets greeted visitors early in the exhibit, some made from black ash splints, others from sweetgrass, birch bark, or porcupine. They ranged from the first half of the century to the 1970s. Stories accompanied them, one of a girl who started making baskets when she was four years old. She helped her parents peddle baskets around the resort to make their living. One woman promised her granddaughter that she would make baskets until she could afford to bring her home from school for her vacation.

Entering another area, I sat on the floor and placed my coffee cup and tote bag beside me. I took notes with my journal in my lap and Rocky's *Eye of the Tiger* theme playing in the background. In the 1880s, American Indians were often featured performers, paid to be "Indians." Their role was to act as opponents for cowboy performers who would defend the "marauding Indians" to the delight of the crowds. Like Arab Americans, natives were encouraged to act in stereotypes that caused others to view their culture as inferior, primitive, and uncivilized. The popular images often needed to be corrected and were only part of their story. By the early 1900s, the early popular images of Indians were that of rustic people who lived unchanged from their historical past.

I stared at the words ringing through the exhibit: We had to change in response to pressures from non-Indian settlements.

Our people learned new ways to make a living. Because of discrimination, jobs open to the Anishinabek were often low paying and seasonal. Schools tried to stamp out Indian culture. Children at government schools were often punished for speaking their native language or practicing traditional customs. Strict discipline and military-style uniforms erased native culture and replaced it with Western habits. In 1828, we had to become Europeanized or removed from the land. We became mostly Roman Catholics, and when the black robes came with the cross, it was considered a good thing because the cross represented the four directions. Our ability to adjust to change let us stay in Michigan.

I considered my people in their native land, how we were, and still are, considered second-class citizens. The difference between the natives of Iraq and Native Americans is that in America, natives were able to win some wars. They had maintained a much stronger presence in their native land than we could. They could insert their rights, tell their stories, and gain reparations. We have not. They are encouraged to criticize their oppressors, despite their oppressors' attempts to reconcile the past. We are not.

We lost our land and our ability to share or continue our stories in our native lands. No one has or likely ever will take accountability for what happened or pay reparations. In our new country, many face resistance from telling the truth of their experiences for fear of offending the oppressors. So we must suppress, defend, or skirt our traumas, pains, and sorrows.

I remembered the US invasions of Iraq. Once I'd asked

the Oneida Man, "Do you think people learned anything from the Vietnam War?"

"Yeah. There's a lot more hate for people of color," he said, then asked, "What do you mean, if people learned a lesson?"

"Well, the 2003 war on Iraq—people supported that even though they saw the senselessness of the Vietnam War."

"Look at it this way. Your daughter did poorly in school. Can't get a job, except at McDonald's or as a housecleaner. So they go to the army, get healthcare and a paycheck. Otherwise, your child won't be hired cause they don't have blond hair. Same with black people—you're not going to work in my office, but you can join the army. And if in the army, you don't do what you're told, you're first in line in friendly fire and you come home in a coffin. You're a hero, but you're not alive. I had a friend telling me there's more people in the platoon killed by friendly fire than by the enemy. The only way you're a hero is if you get shot."

I told him the story of the Halabja massacre, a chemical attack carried by the Iraqi government on March 16, 1988, during the Iran-Iraq War. Halabja is a Kurdish city located in northern Iraq near the Iranian border. The attack killed an estimated 5,000 people and the international community widely condemned it. But a colleague of mine who'd served on the front line told me a different version of the story. Amer Hanna Fatuhi is an artist, historian and activist who fled Iraq due to political persecution. He claims that the attack was intended at Iran's enemy line, not Halabja. A gust of wind came out of nowhere and blew it in the wrong direction.

"The story shifted the same way the wind did," said the

Oneida Man. "As a parent, you don't like seeing your child killing people, but you still love them and wish they return alive. It's silly. They have toys and they have to play with them. That's how friendly fire happens. If you cause an effect, then you need to be able to take care of the cause-and-effect too because it's going to affect you. If you can't handle it, you'll probably die. If you call in the dark dance, you better have groceries because it'll affect you too. There's nothing precise about war. Nobody knows the outcome."

I gathered my stuff and stood, then continued to stroll through the exhibit, observing how the Anishinabek relied on natural materials. Eva Petoskey from Peshawbestown wrote, "The sky, the sun, the stars, the moon, the rocks, the earth, this water, the plants, the trees have always been the teachers of the Anishinabek." An arrow incorporated leather, wood, stone, and deer sinew. Personal symbols identified the owner of items, many of which were animal symbols indicating one's spirit helper, name, or clan.

I stared at a display of pink shawls that represented traditional teachings and individual experiences. They embodied the warmth, protection, and love given by women as they cared for people in their immediate circle, extended family, and all people generally. A child ran into the exhibit, clapping and then shouting. Someone said something to him, and he responded, "What?!" There was silence, followed by more shouting. Another child walked in and, looking around, said, "This is scary!"

"Scary?" his mother asked.

"Yeah, it's so quiet."

"Well, it's a museum."

The next time I went to Haraz Coffee, it felt odd. The place was nearly empty. It didn't take long to remember that we're in Ramadan, the holy month of fasting for Muslims. They fast from sunrise to sunset and abstain from consuming caffeine and smoking, though not everyone abides by this sacred tradition that predates Islam. The Hebrew Bible and New Testament mention fasting from food and drink to reach a heightened spiritual level by constantly remembering God. People detach from worldly desires to pay attention to their inner selves, become more grateful, and do good deeds such as donating to charities and feeding the hungry. Ramadan comes from the Arabic word "the hot month," when God revealed the Quran, Islam's holy book, to Muhammad.

The place did not feel right without the hustle and bustle that resembled the homes and streets of the Arab world, which I had grown accustomed to at Haraz. The servers had their eyes glued to their phones. It must be challenging for them to fast during this time. The Arabic song playing sounded louder than usual. Was it because they raised the volume or because of the absence of people talking? I don't know, but the heartfelt songs by unknown artists touched me, and I couldn't stop thinking of the olden days. I looked outside and watched two women veiled from top to bottom with long abayas walk to their car, one carrying a baby. I think of Baghdad. I keep traveling to the past, then the future, and then returning to the present, like someone riding an airplane, constantly taking off and landing.

My husband sent me a text with a picture of the Chaldean News. Circled were my names beside two recently published articles, one categorized under "Celebrating Chaldean Heritage," where I interviewed Amanda Podany, professor and author of *Weavers, Scribes, and Kings*. I wipe away a few tears and return to my notes. I had a conversation with the Oneida Man a few years ago after returning from my spiritual and writing conference and retreat, the Path of Consciousness, an idea inspired by a tiny hidden place in Mexico.

"Hi, how are you?" I asked.

"I'm returning your call."

"Yes, I see."

"Are you there?" he asked.

"Where, on earth?"

"What?"

"On earth?"

"Oh," he said, laughing. "No, in cyberspace."

"Yes. I'm there often and sometimes on earth."

We laughed.

"So, how are you?" he asked.

"I lost my voice. I did this retreated and worked so hard on autopilot, and then I crashed when I got home."

"You need to use more ESP—Extra Sensory Perception—instead of talking so much at these conferences. It's funny, my dad told me before that when you visit with somebody, someone that's a very good friend, you can sit for five minutes, and you don't say anything, and it doesn't matter. Some people chit-chat so much, you know what I mean, and then they feel bad if they're not talking. But really good friends don't have to do that. That's when extra sensory perception kicks in. You get onto the same page with someone. It's hard to do that at a conference with many people." There was a pause. "Are you there?" he asked.

"Yes, I'm listening to you. My voice is resting."

"Well, I won't keep you long."

He jumped from various topics, including diabetes, carjacking, and kids who behave like little devils. "They say it's learned. No, it's in kids to begin with. Kids say anything, and they don't care. We're born not really nice people, brand new out of the box, shitting and peeing all over you, and they don't care. That's basically what it's like. You have to learn to be nice, tolerant and know what to say and not say. In other words, you can't blame everything on your parents. When you go see the Creator, it's personal. You're not going to go with your Daddy or Mommy. You're going to meet the Creator yourself. People always try to make a reason why or an excuse, but no. Young people have to learn how to behave in society and who to hang around with or not hang around with."

A bookmark came to mind that says, "10 ways to raise a responsible child." It talked about establishing family rules, giving chores to do, praising your child for completing responsibilities, teaching them good health and safety habits, making it your children's responsibility to get their homework done on time, and other things. At the bottom, it says, "Remember—children learn by what they see and hear. Set a good example. Act responsibly."

The bookmark is placed inside *Memoirs of a Babylonian Princess* by Maria Theresa Asmar, a Chaldean woman from my parents' ancestral village Tel Keppe. In her two-part memoir series, she writes about her people, the Chaldeans, and what she and they suffered in the hands of the Ottoman rule. She travels alone to other countries in the Middle East and Europe. Given her background and dedication to her people through writing and education, she reminds me a lot of myself.

"What did you do with your hair?" I asked, taking the conversation in another direction.

"Threw it in the garbage."

"Why didn't you donate it?"

"They do that with horsehair to make shoe brushes."

"What's shoe brush?"

"To polish your shoes. You're probably a throwaway type of girl. Throw it out when your boots are old." I said I was the opposite of that, and he then explained what shoe brush is used for and how it's used in the army. I knew what a shoe brush was but had associated donating hair to children of cancer, as we did with my son's hair once it grew to ten inches.

We somehow circled to the topic of his death, how he had died four times but lived, nonetheless. I again asked him what that felt like.

"My sister tried to investigate this about my death," he said. "I told her it was personal. I can't describe what happened. Each person has a personal experience with the Creator. It's between you as a human and the Creator." He paused for a moment. "One thing I know is that this place here is so slow. Life is so slow. When I wasn't here, things were exceptionally faster. I didn't want to come back. There was no reason, but there was. It just wasn't my reason. It's up to us to do the best we can do here, but when the time comes, it's not up to us. People think they can kill themselves. They can't kill themselves because the Creator will stand you up again if it's not your time. There's a lot of controversy about that—what do you call that?"

"Suicide."

"Yes, suicide. You can't even do that by yourself. I don't think so. There are times when you can't do it. That's what I tried to tell my sister anyway. It's not black or white. It's more spiritual than not spiritual. But people think they can do that. They can leave if they want and stay if they want. You're connected to so much stuff that you can't do it when you want to. You are spiritual, no matter what. Then you get people who say, 'I'm an atheist. I don't believe in God.' Then you step on their toe, and they say, "Oh my God!' First thing they do is holler God's name." He laughed and continued, "No matter what you call yourself, you still believe in God, no matter what you call God. And some people think God is a woman, and I don't think God is a man or a woman. It's an entity, not a person."

The night we'd toured the Grand Rapids Public Museum, my husband and I sat in our hotel room and watched a show about ancient aliens on the History Channel. They discussed a ceramic bowl with Sumerian cuneiform that a local farmer discovered in the 1950s near Tiahuanaco and Lake Titicaca. Tiahuanaco is said to be the most significant Native American civilization that many people haven't heard of.

Researchers worldwide believe that the bowl, known as the Fuente Magna Bowl, provides proof of otherworldly contact at Puma Punku, a large archaeological complex in Bolivia. They ask, "Is it possible that the Sumerians are related to Bolivia?" Were there beings all around the earth who had Godlike powers and could perform miracles? That there were architects who could access cosmic information, which some have kept hidden and kept a secret?

It seems that no matter where we look, we see a universal cosmic truth that belongs to everyone. It is not reserved for one tribe. Virlana Tkacz writes, "Some scholars believe that White Shamanism contains fragments of an old Mesopotamian religion brought to this area thousands of years ago… The earliest worshipers of a god of the Heavens were the ancient Sumerians… It is our opinion that what is known as White Shamanism in central Asia was brought by ancient immigrants from southwestern Asia."

Countless developments and inventions originated in ancient Mesopotamia, including writing and the wheel. Yet few people give thought to their origins. That does not mean that Iraqis should say, "Sorry, you can't use this type of communication or method of transportation. Find your own." Ancient teachings have survived because their form changes along with time, and no one has ownership over them, except for the Creator.

We are all natives of this land, though we forget that part of us. Our identity is consciousness. The truth is encoded in our DNA, but our programming of over 5000 years needs major upgrading to unlock the secrets we have forgotten. As women and men, we are awakening, realizing no one is more or less than another, though we have among us the wise ones and the fools.

I recalled the objects and displays at the museum of decorative arts, handmade baskets, pink shawls, old photographs, documents handed down through their families, and video interviews with elders and others. How the Anishinabek shared their personal stories and their views about the past, present, and future reminded me of the Chaldean Museum in Michigan and the projects I'd started there, believing that doing projects individually or as a community is an ultimate gift for the universe. I remembered a sign that read, "To all those who joined in preserving this story, we say, 'Megweich... Thank you!'"

I, too, express the same sentiments to those who have welcomed us to this land, helped heal the wounds of yesterdays, and prodded us to tell our stories. In Aramaic, we say, "Gianookhon baseemta... Bless your souls."

CHAPTER 12

New Beginnings

My husband drove three miles on a dirt road that led to a soybean farm. We arrived at a home under renovation tucked behind rows of trees. He pulled into its dirt driveway. A man sat on a chair under the sun, smiling at us. Who is this guy, I wondered. Could this be the Oneida Man? It couldn't be, could it? The Oneida Man was toothless, on the thin side, and had dark skin. This man had sparkling straight white teeth, a buzz cut, and a little belly; his skin color was as white as Lynn's.

"Come on, guys," I said to my seventeen-year-old daughter and my fourteen-year-old son. They stepped out of the car grudgingly, one carrying Teddy and the other holding a cooler that contained snacks, drinks, and a dog's water bowl.

"Hey there," said the Oneida Man, and staring more closely, I realized it was him!

"I didn't recognize you," I said, surprised.

"I've cut my hair," he said, forgetting I'd seen him since he did that. We'd had several conversations about it.

I said nothing and waved to my husband. Assured I was at the right home, he backed out of the driveway. I turned to the Oneida Man. "He drove us here since it's an hour away,"

I said. "He's going to visit a cousin at a nearby store and pick us up in an hour."

Two miniature-fenced goats caught my attention.

"Oh, those are so cute!" I walked in that direction with Teddy on a leash. One of the goats stood mightily over a small plastic igloo. Teddy tried to stick his head into a square patterned fence opening. The Oneida Man had never met Teddy. The last time he'd seen my children was exactly nine years ago when I'd visited him at the junkyard. That day, in August of 2014, we witnessed a protest against the genocide committed by ISIS on our ancestral villages in northern Iraq. Back then, my children were shorter than me, whereas now they are much taller than me. My mother was alive and living with us. Teddy hadn't yet joined our family.

"The grass has puddles because of the heavy rain yesterday," he said, strolling behind me. "There are apple trees and pear trees along that path. There are flower bushes and blackberry bushes. It had gone wild by the previous owners. Of course, I have to pick the berries every day, which takes an hour. Cutting the grass takes another hour. It's ten acres of lawn. That's just what I do. It's retirement. We're all retired here, so it's like an old-age home." He laughed.

"What do you do in the winter?" I asked.

"Stay warm."

He said he now has a bigger home. It's twenty-two feet long and has house windows and house doors. The previous home was twelve feet and was a camper. His brother took it and sold it.

"The new home is not that big, but it's enough for me,"

he said. "I joke that if I had a female friend, that would be her makeup room, and I would have to find another place to stay." His voice was the only thing that was the same as before.

"You look good, younger than before," I said.

"I spend a lot of time out here, more than in the house. We have a pond in the back with lots of fish. It's hard to go back there with the puddles. Otherwise, I have a fishing pole for your son. Maybe he could catch a few fish."

He said the young people in their family come with dirt bikes, four-wheelers, etc. "It's an inexpensive outing," he said.

"You have your own family retreat."

"Yeah, they come here and have fun."

"We're going to walk through this path," I said, pointing at the trees.

"Okay," he said. "I can't come with you because I'll start running out of breath. I'm an old man now, man." He laughed. "This is an old folks' home."

Staring at him, the younger version of him, the man who used to visit the video store, flashed before my eyes. He was active back then, going in and out of the store and across the parking lot with steps as quick as a rabbit's. Now he could barely take a few steps.

Led by Teddy, my children and I walked between the trees. Our feet sunk into the watery grass. My children made jokes about not having worn the right shoes for this venture. They ate some of their snacks. They complained. The Oneida Man followed us with a green lawnmower tractor a little later.

He parked the vehicle and stepped down. He pointed to the rows of soybeans and said that his sister leased that land.

The owner came once to plant the soybeans and once to pick the harvest with heavy equipment. "There's a shooting range there," he said, gesturing near an empty white bench table. "When the kids come over, we set up tents and sleep."

"No animals come out?"

"Deer and sometimes coyote," he said. "You can hear them howling in packs, but they are far away. They can be dangerous, though. We have pheasants, rabbits, and look, here are deer hoof prints." He lowered to touch freshly made hoof prints.

"Oh yeah," said my children, approaching the site.

We looked around and took in the sun and natural air as he, sitting in his vehicle, told us about the apple and pear trees, the flower and blackberry bushes, the over fifty acres of soybeans, the shooting range, the pond, and the animals. We decided to walk back to the house and sit. The Oneida Man drove ahead of us. When we got there, I told my son to pour water into a bowl for Teddy. As he did that, I saw the Oneida Man's sister come outside. Nine years ago, she was the one who'd said, "I see you have new additions." Her husband has since passed away.

She had a cigarette in one hand. Her long silver hair with slight waves flowed around her. She looked like a full-figured elderly mermaid, though younger than before. Even the Oneida Man seemed to have trimmed off ten years from his appearance. I couldn't get over the change.

They had us enter the vast garage, where an eight-chair cherrywood dining table greeted us. Stacked against the walls were boxes and random small furniture pieces. We sat around the table. The reversible swing cushions across from me, layered on each other like Legos, caught my attention. They were striped on one side, flowery on the other, and the same as what we had on our swing at home.

"You guys look really good," I said.

"It's being out here in nature," she said.

"You're even a lot lighter," I told the Oneida Man.

"I was dark from working in the sun all day and from the oil and grease in the junkyard that stained my skin," he said. "It was so darn hard to get it off, even in the shower. Then you're back out and get it all over your skin again, so it never really leaves you."

We chitchatted about the video store, gas station, the shopping center where they used to stop, the people who worked there, still do, and those who have moved on. We brought up my mom and their mom and her delicious rhubarb cake.

"I met your mom," said the Oneida Man.

"You did?" I asked.

"Yeah. One day you called me from the airport and needed a ride home. I picked you up and dropped you off. I saw your mom from a distance. She stood at the door, waiting for you."

"Yes, that was her," I said, remembering how she always looked out for me. But I could not remember him ever picking me up from anywhere let alone an airport. Perhaps he was losing his sanity, or perhaps it was I who was losing mine.

We talked about the similarities between our communities and the differences. The sister asked me about my childhood, coming here at a young age, and the culture shock I must have experienced. I told her in the past, I felt bad about having to leave my birth country. When I got older, I understood how lucky I was to come to the United States.

"I know what you mean," she said. "I was so happy to get off the reservation. It was terrible there, just terrible. Never want to go back there."

"It's a place where people go to die," said the Oneida Man. "It's all doom and despair."

I had to admit that, though Iraq had a special place in my heart, decades of seeing our communities swept out of that region has killed any feelings of wanting to reconnect with that land. A few weeks prior, on August 3 and around the ninth anniversary of ISIS' attacks on our ancestral villages, I attended a hybrid talk at the University College of London by Dr. Salah Al Jabari. He is the Director of UNESCO Chair for Genocide Prevention Studies in the Islamic World. For over an hour, he focused on the Shia genocide, briefly mentioning the Yezidis in Iraq. He did not say a word about Christians.

Once Salah finished his talk, the organizer asked if anyone had questions. I typed in the chat box: Why didn't the speaker mention a word about the Christians? The United States had announced ISIS' atrocities against the Shia, Yazidis, and Christians as a genocide. Salah's first reason was that Christians' genocide was less important than others, followed by other causes of displacement, diaspora, etc., all of which infuriated me.

I messaged the organizer, "How could he claim one genocide is less important than another? How was such a biased person given this kind of position? He lectured for over an hour about the significance of the Islamic World embracing diversity and how we must acknowledge past wrongs to avoid repeating them. He had said all the politically correct things, yet his actions had shown his true racist intentions. The organizer did not share these truths with the speaker.

The following day, I emailed UNESCO (in France) and UNESCO Genocide Prevention (in New York), explaining what happened. I reminded them that Christians have endured unparalleled persecution throughout history which led to their displacement on a global scale. The relentless and tragic oppression and disregard for their appeals for humanitarian rights have persisted over the course of several decades, giving rise to the underlying issues that have led to massacres in 1914, 1933, 1968, and most recently, 2014. Any prospects of attaining their rightful and fair rights have significantly diminished, causing a continuous decline in their population. The massacres inflicted upon our people have left a lasting impact on their lives and communities. The sense of stability and belonging that once existed has been shattered, and for many, the process of rebuilding their lives has become an arduous and challenging task.

UNESCO has not yet responded.

I shared what Salah had done with my friends and colleagues who range from Christians, Jews, Muslims, and other faiths. They agreed that for someone in Dr. Jabar's position to brush Christians' persecution and genocide under the carpet is troubling and wrong. He's supposed to work towards a world where all forms of genocide are recognized and prevented. There was one Chaldean who rationalized his biased action with sym(pathetic) intellectual observations, saying, "Every group remembers their own."

Uh, no. Not when that person holds the position of

Director of UNESCO Chair for Genocide Prevention Studies in the Islamic World. In my book *Witnessing a Genocide*, published in 2015, I included the genocide against the Christians, Yazidis, Shia, Sunni, Kurds, and others. When you truly believe in humanity, you don't play favorites. You see the situation for what it is, and the truth is, the Shia, whom Salah focused on, is currently the largest population of Iraq. They have been in power since 2003. The constitution of Iraq establishes Islam as the official religion and states that no law may be enacted, contradicting the "established provisions of Islam."

In the month prior to Salah's talk, the Iraqi president revoked a decree that recognized Louis Sako as the Chaldean patriarch in the country. So, the patriarch left his residence in Baghdad and relocated to a monastery in northern Kurdistan. According to the Iraqi Christian Foundation, the Chaldean leadership last fled Baghdad when a Mongol army was hardening its control of the city in 1259 A.D. Sako's departure had many effects, including losing control over the church's assets and properties.

A text ping brought me out of my head. My son, who sat on the right-side corner of the table, sent me a message. "Where is Babba at LMKKK?"

We had called my husband to tell him to pick us up. We asked that he bring along food from his cousin's store: pizza, chicken wings, breadsticks, and, of course, don't forget the sauce. While we waited, the kids took over the conversation. They made fun of how, at home, when my husband and I wanted something, we called them on the iPhone and said, "Come here."

"They could just tell us what they want on the phone," my son said, laughing.

"Yeah, and my mom, when she wants to tell my brother something, she'll tell me to call him when he's right in his room," my daughter said.

In my opinion, they were fabricating and exaggerating the scenarios. But who could argue with two teenagers?

My children had no recollection of when I'd taken them to the junkyard nine years prior. They don't remember ever meeting the Oneida Man. I was surprised. I'd written about that experience so many times in several of my books that I assumed it was ingrained in their memory as well as mine.

I got another text. My husband had arrived. We got up, gathered our stuff, and headed to the car. The Oneida Man and his sister followed us. When my husband saw them, he stepped out of the car and approached us, extending his hand out as I introduced them.

"It's beautiful here," my husband said, looking around.

"It's our old-folk retirement home," said the Oneida Man, smiling.

"I told Weam we should find a house like this to retire into," said my husband.

"You're welcome to come and hang out here. Go fishing in the pond," the Oneida Man said. He then showed us a picture of his brother-in-law holding a big bass half his size.

"Were you guys able to eat it?" I asked.

"Yeah, we cooked and ate it," he said, laughing.

"I mean, because of the water."

"The pond fish are safe for consumption," his sister said.

THE ONEIDA MAN

My husband exchanged a few more words and said it was nice to meet them. Then he and the children got into the car. I stood before the Oneida Man and his sister, observing the decades that had passed with us in each other's lives. I wondered if I'd ever see them again. Was this the end or the start of a new beginning?

I hugged the sister, and as I pulled away, she kissed me on the left cheek. She reminded me of one of my sisters, not by appearance but by character. I shook the Oneida Man's hand and left towards the car.

We drove away into the dirt road. The kids in the back raved about the amount and variety of food their cousin sent them. They dug into the pizza, fries, and chicken nuggets but left alone the chicken wings. "They're too messy to eat in the car," my daughter said. Hungry, I asked them to pass me the fries, chicken nuggets, and pizza. We ate while Teddy lounged between my son and daughter, panting. We all got full.

"By the way, what is LMKKK?" I asked my son.

"What?" he asked.

"The text you sent me. What does LMKKK stand for?"

"Oh my God, mom, you don't know?" he said.

"It stands for Let Me Know," my daughter said.

"Why three Ks?" I asked.

"That's an emphasis on the *know*," she said.

I smiled and stared out the window. All around us there's a history that's unknown. It will fade away unless we search for and uncover the truth. I closed my eyes. The long stretches of trees and land hypnotized me into a sleepy state. LMKKK flashed repeatedly in my head.

NOTES

Introduction

The Racial Slur Database rsdb.org/races

Niki Foster, "Why Are Native Americans Called Indians?" *Historical Index*, (June 19, 2023) www.historicalindex.org/why-are-native-americans-called-indians.htm

Weam Namou, "Love, Justice, and Turtle Soup" *SN Review* www.snreview.org/0210Namou.html

Chapter 1

C. Thomas, *Report on the Mound Explorations of the Bureau of Ethnology* (1894, report. 1985)

Chapter 2

Brian Sheets, "Papers or Plastic: The Difficulty in Protecting Native Spiritual Identity," (April 22, 2013) *Lewis & Clark Law Review* Vol. 17, No. 2, pg. 596

Gary Hobson, "The Rise of the White Shaman as a New Version of Cultural Imperialism" *The Remembered Earth*, Albuquerque, NM: Red Earth Press, 1978: pg. 100—108

Chapter 3

Timothy Doran, *Women in the Hellenistic World: Issues, Evidence and Conclusions*, University of California Press, 2011

Merlin Stone, When God Was a Woman: The Dial Press, New York, 1976: pg. 15

Ibid, pg. 23

Chapter 4

Adhid Miri, PhD, "Cardinal Sako Stands Against Conquest and Confiscation" The Chaldean News, (July 15, 2023)

Chapter 5

Ancient Shamans
www.templeoftheola.org/ancient-shamans.html

Chapter 6

Robert Shaw, Historical Origins, comprising "The Chaldaean Hebrew and Chinese and Hindoo origins," St. Louis Becktold & Company, 1889 (pg. 6)

Maria Theresa Asmar, Memoirs of a Babylonian Princess, G.B. Zieber & Company, Philadelphia, 1845 (pg. 29)

Chapter 7

"First Farmers: 4,000 Years of Indigenous Michigan Horticulture," Michigan State University Museum September 23, 2012—November 30, 2012 museum.msu.edu/?exhibition=michigans-first-farmers-4000-years-of-indigenous-michigan-horticulture

Roger Sutherland, "A Taste of Beekeeping History", Ypsilanti Gleanings, Winter 2012

"A Brief History of Honey," Meridian Hive
meridianhive.com/blogs/blog/a-brief-history-of-honey

Chapter 8

Bethan McKernan and Hussein al-Yabari, "From khat to coffee: revitalising an age-old Yemeni crop," The Guardian, Feb. 14, 2020

Romeo Historical Society
romeohistoricalsociety.org/history/

Jessica Mendoza, "Why is ISIS destroying ancient artifacts in Iraq?" Christian Science Monitor, February 2015

Chapter 10

Clyde Winters, "Was Bolivia-Peru the Sunset Land of the Sumerians?" Ancient Origins (September 2016)

Virlana Tkacz, Siberian Shamanism: The Shanar Ritual of the Buryats, New Edition of Shanar (January 2016)

Chapter 11

Nahrein Network Youtube Channel—Genocide Studies in Iraq and the work of the UNESCO Chair for Genocide Prevention Studies (August 7, 2023)

Adhid Miri, PhD, "Cardinal Sako Stands Against Conquest and Confiscation" The Chaldean News, (July 15, 2023)